Robert E. Lee

A tribute to General Lee from the author of the *"Battle Hymn of the Republic."*

ROBERT E. LEE

A gallant foeman in the fight,
    A brother when the fight was o'er,
The hand that led the host with might
    The blessed torch of learning bore.

No shriek of shells nor roar of drums,
    No challenge fierce, resounding far,
When reconciling Wisdom comes
    To heal the cruel wounds of war.

Thought may the minds of man divide,
    Love makes the heart of nations one,
And so, thy soldier grave beside,
    We honor thee, Virginia's son.

Julia Ward Howe

Books by Colonel Harold B. Simpson

AS AUTHOR

Brawling Brass—North and South (1960)
Gaines' Mill to Appomattox (1963)
Fort Mason, Texas *(Frontier Forts of Texas)* (1966)

AS AUTHOR/EDITOR

Touched With Valor (1964)

AS EDITOR

First Texas Infantry Regiment, CSA (1964)
The Bugle Softly Blows (1965)
Texas in the War, 1861-1865 (1965)
Robert E. Lee (1966)

Robert E Lee

By

Jefferson Davis

Edited and with an Introduction and Notes
by
COLONEL HAROLD B. SIMPSON

Published
by
THE HILL JUNIOR COLLEGE PRESS

To the United States Military Academy at
West Point and two of its most illustrious graduates, Robert Edward Lee and Jefferson Davis.

Acknowledgments

Dr. W. Lamar Fly, President of Hill Junior College, for his encouragement and interest.

The Board of Regents of Hill Junior College: Mr. Ollie Baker (President), Mr. Joseph Campbell, Mrs. Dick Cason, Mr. Donald Eastland, Mr. Odis Gray, Mrs. Miller Herrington, Mr. Wallace Lavender, Mr. John Standefer, and Mr. James Sumner, for their financial support and enthusiastic backing.

Misses Paulla Fair and Jere Hamilton for typing, proof-reading and indexing.

Mr. Charles King, Chairman of the English Department, McLennan County Junior College, Waco, Texas, for his suggested corrections and additions.

Mr .Kenneth W. Rapp, Assistant Archivist of the United States Military Academy, West Point, New York for information on Cadets Robert E. Lee and Jefferson Davis.

Dr. W. C. Nunn, a great admirer of Robert E. Lee and Professor of Southern History at Texas Christian University, for his enthusiasm and inspiration.

Mr. Robert E. Davis (Texian Press) and Mr. Frank Jasek (Library Binding Co.) for their guidance and suggestions on layout, printing, and binding.

Fred Jones, Milo Beesley, Ray Badley, Earl and Jimmy Davis and Clarence Kedrowski, outstanding artisans and technicians of the printing and bookbinding profession.

My appreciation and thanks to them all.

Contents

Acknowledgements -- vi

Introduction --- ix

Robert E. Lee by Jefferson Davis -------------------------------------- 1

Portfolio of Selected Photographs
of Robert E. Lee -- Follows 12

Notes and References -- 13

Appendix -- 69

Bibliography -- 73

Index -- 75

Illustrations

of

R O B E R T E. L E E

All Illustrations follow Page 12

First Known Photograph (with son "Rooney"), 1845

In the Uniform of a Captain of Engineers, 1846

As a Brevet Colonel in Civilian Clothes, 1850 or 1851

Only Photograph Taken in the Field, 1862

First Formally Posed Photograph as the Commander of
the Army of Northern Virginia, 1863

Much Copied Left Full Profile Photograph, 1864

Lee's Favorite Photograph, 1864

First Photograph Taken on Traveller, 1864

After Appomattox—in Richmond, April 16, 1865

The General, son Custis and Colonel Walter Taylor, 1865

Left Full Profile by Brady, 1865

On Traveller, 1866

Brady Photograph Taken in Washington, 1869

Rare Full Right Profile, 1869 or 1870

With Joseph E. Johnston, 1870

Death Mask, October 12, 1870

Introduction

Jefferson Davis, just before his death on December 6, 1889, wrote a study of Robert E. Lee for *The North American Review,* one of the more sophisticated monthly journals of the nineteenth century. Davis' article appeared in the January, 1890 issue of *The Review* and was probably the last formal piece of writing to come from the pen of the former Confederate President. The staff of *The Review* was in possession of Mr. Davis' study of Lee shortly before his death and printed it the following month with the permission of Mrs. Davis. The study also appeared (with permission from *The Review*) in volume seventeen of the *Southern Historical Society Papers* published at Richmond. This volume of the *Southern Papers,* although dated 1889, did not appear in print until the spring of 1890.

Except for short references to General Lee's life, character, and military ability in his previously published work, this is the only lengthy treatment of the leader of the famed Army of Northern Virginia written by his commander in chief, the President of the Confederate States. Millions of words have found their way into print concerning the life and services of Robert E. Lee. Except for Washington and Lincoln (and possibly Grant), more lines have been written about this great Southern soldier than about any other American. Americans and foreigners, relatives and strangers, soldiers and civilians, and people representing all degrees of authority and competence have composed tens of biographies of the outstanding Virginian. The value of these works ranges from the definitive and magnificent four-volume masterpiece by Douglas Southall Freeman, entitled simply *R. E. Lee,* to the highly emotional, imaginative, and inaccurate one-volume work by John E. Hobeika called *Lee, the Soul of Honor: An Appreciation by an Orientalist with Additional Facts.*

Now added to the studies of Lee in book form is this short, interesting, and revealing biography. It is written by a person who, in many respects, was in a better position to evaluate Robert E. Lee than any other man—Jefferson Davis, fellow cadet, friend, commander in chief. Freeman, who was most critical of the printed sources on Lee, has called this study by Davis "an estimate of value."[1] What it lacks in quantity it makes up in quality.

Jefferson Davis and Robert E. Lee first became acquainted

in 1825, the year that Lee entered West Point. Davis had entered the Academy the year before. By coincidence both cadets had been recommended for appointment to the Military Academy by the great South Carolina statesman, John C. Calhoun.[2] Davis was graduated with the Class of 1828; Lee, with the Class of 1829.

While a cadet on the Hudson, Lee compiled a much more impressive record than did Davis. The Virginian ranked number two in a class of forty-six[3] and was one of the few cadets in the long history of West Point to be graduated without a single demerit. Lee served as a cadet assistant professor of mathematics his third (sophomore) and second (junior) class years, and when a first classman (senior) he was selected as the adjutant of the Corps of Cadets. Robert E. Lee was designated a "Distinguished Cadet" at the end of each of the four academic years—an honor bestowed on only the highest five cadets in relative class standing.[4] Upon graduation in 1829, Cadet Lee was commissioned a brevet second lieutenant in the corps of engineers, the branch of service usually reserved for the top graduates. Lee's subsequent military career in the United States Army was long and distinguished. His work as an engineer was outstanding. His record in the Mexican War was brilliant. Lee resigned from the United States Army on April 20, 1861, after almost thirty-two years of dedicated service.

Davis' military record was much more distinguished after he left the Academy than it was while he was a cadet. He was graduated number twenty-three in a class of thirty-three in 1828.[5] He served in the regular army until 1835, when he resigned his commission and eloped with the daughter of General (and future President) Zachary Taylor. During his seven-year regular army stint in the infantry and dragoons, Lieutenant Davis was stationed on the Northwest frontier and saw action in the Blackhawk War (1832-33). Upon the outbreak of the Mexican War, Davis resigned his congressional seat to organize and lead the 1st Mississippi Rifles, an elite volunteer regiment from the Magnolia State. Colonel Davis and his regiment won battle honors at Buena Vista (February 22-23, 1847). The Mississippian was painfully wounded in the battle and saw no more action during the war. He declined a brigadier general's star in the regular army following the war and chose instead to pursue his political career.[6] Jefferson Davis served as the Secretary of War for Franklin Pierce (1853-57) and is considered to have been one of the ablest men to fill that key cabinet post.

The relationship between Lee and Davis was very close at times and always friendly, although some historians have attempted to build a barrier between the two. In each situation where Davis and Lee came into close personal relationship with each other, Davis always held the superior position. At West Point the Mississippian was one class ahead of the Virginian. When Lee was superintendent of the Military Academy, Davis was Secretary of War; and during the Civil War Jefferson Davis occupied the chief executive's chair as commander in chief, while Robert E. Lee commanded one of the Confederate armies. This constant difference in relative position probably accounts for the deference that Lee showed for Davis throughout their association.

Because of their long acquaintance it would be natural that some informality might have existed between the two by the 1860's regardless of the formal command line relationship, but this was not the case. Lee always maintained a formal, official courtesy in all of his correspondence with Davis. During the war, he addressed the chief executive usually as "Mr. President" or "Your Excellency" and nearly always signed himself "Your obedient servant." There is no reason to doubt but that the conversations between the two followed the same pattern. Davis was almost as formal with Lee, but he did relax the stiffness of his relationship somewhat in his famous letter to Lee on August 11 when he referred to the Virginian as "my dear friend."[7]

President Davis, who could be blunt and impatient at times, probably hurt the feelings of General Lee and provoked him on several occasions. However, Lee, with his superb self-control, politeness, and tact, would not permit the President's unguarded remarks and hasty actions to impair their long-standing friendship. Only once during the war was this harmonious relationship threatened.

According to Douglas Southall Freeman, who seemingly has researched every minute detail of Lee's life, the nearest approach to an open break between the two occurred during late January or early February, 1865. The end of the Confederacy was near, tempers were taut, and friends were finicky. The incident was generated by an exchange of correspondence concerning the destruction of tobacco in the Richmond warehouses to keep it from falling into the hands of the Federals.

Davis telegraphed Lee: "Rumor said to be based on orders

given by you create concern and obstruct necessary legislation. Come over. I wish to have your views on the subject."

Lee replied that it was difficult to leave Petersburg and concluded his telegram with, "Send me the measures [legislation], and I shall send you my views."

Davis regarded the reply as flippant and angrily shot back a lengthy, cutting message that ended: "Rest assured I will not ask your views in answer to measures [legislation]. Your counsels are no longer wanted in this matter."[8]

Lee immediately had Traveller saddled and rode to Richmond to see the President. The personal interview that followed apparently soothed the ruffled feathers; for a few days later, on February 6, 1865, President Davis named Lee to the newly created post of General in Chief of the Armies of the Confederate States.[9]

Although Davis entered into bitter controversies with several of his top generals (Joseph E. Johnston, P. G. T. Beauregard and D. H. Hill being prime examples), his association with Lee was on the highest and most cordial plane. The President was a man of extreme likes and dislikes when dealing with individuals. Classmates and Mexican War acquaintances like Braxton Bragg and John C. Pemberton and young tigers and flatterers like John Bell Hood seemingly could do no wrong, while the trio of "Davis Outcasts"—Johnston, Beauregard and D. H. Hill—could do nothing right.

Davis admired Lee tremendously, set him apart from all other Confederate generals, and interfered with his military operations surprisingly little (although he differed with Lee quite often). The President realized that the great popularity of Lee after the summer of 1862 made the General immune to presidential criticism and disfavor of any sort. Some historians have attempted to show that beneath the calm surface of the president-general relationship there existed a seething mass of misunderstanding, malcontent, and mistrust between the two Confederate leaders. Davis was usually pointed out by the writers of this school as the culprit that strained to the breaking point the relations between the two,[10] but it must be remembered that the Confederate President had to contend with numerous unsolvable problems that vexed him constantly and undoubtedly affected his disposition.

As President of the Confederate States, Davis faced a more difficult task than had ever been faced by any American President. His term of office never knew a day of peace; the Confederate States of America were on a wartime footing from the beginning to the end. Davis was constantly plagued by logistical problems from food to manpower that could not be satisfactorily solved. The government was never financially solvent and spiraling inflation riddled the economy. Half of the governors in the strong states rights Confederacy were at the best lukewarm toward Davis and three—Joseph E. Brown (Georgia), Zeb Vance (North Carolina), and Pendleton Murrah (Texas)—were actually hostile. The President was constantly badgered (often unmercifully) by unsympathetic members of the Confederate Congress led by Louis T. Wigfall (Texas), William L. Yancey (Alabama), and Thomas R. R. Cobb (Georgia). It is questionable if even the magnificent and imperturbable Robert E. Lee could have weathered the four-year storm that brewed around the chief executive's office in Richmond.

No challenge in the Confederacy was so difficult as the challenge faced by Jefferson Davis. It is hard to see how anyone at the time could have accomplished more than he did or could have met the challenge more fully than he did.

Long out of print, unavailable and practically unknown, *Robert E. Lee* by Jefferson Davis can be found today in only a few of the largest public and university libraries. The Board of Regents of Hill Junior College has done the public a great service by perpetuating in book form this important study of a great American. The study appears (except for a few corrections in spelling and clarifying additions) exactly as Jefferson Davis wrote it in 1889—a few weeks before his death.

Harold B. Simpson

Hillsboro, Texas   September 15, 1966

---

[1]Douglas Southall Freeman, **R. E. Lee** (4 vols., New York: Charles Scribner's Sons, 1936), IV, 553.

[2]**Ibid.,** I, 45.

[3]The West Point Alumni Foundation, Inc., **Register of Graduates and Former Cadets: United States Military Academy** (New York: West Point Alumni Foundation, 1965), 124. Quoted hereafter as **Register of Graduates.**

[4]Letter to the editor from Kenneth W. Rapp, Assistant Archivist, United States Military Academy, dated 7 December, 1965.

[5]**Register of Graduates, op. cit.,** 123.

[6]Had Davis accepted the star he would have been the first West Point graduate to become a general officer of the line in the regular army.

[7]United States War Department, **War of the Rebellion: Official Records of the Union and Confederate Armies** (128 vols., Washington: U. S. Government Printing Office, 1880-1901), Series I, Volume XXIX, Part II, 640. Quoted hereafter as **O. R.**

[8]Freeman, **op. cit.,** III, 533-34.

[9]**O. R., op. cit.,** Series I, Volume XLVI, Part II, 1205.

[10]"General Lee's Unsolved Problem" by Clifford Dowdey, **American Heritage,** Vol. VI, No. 3 (April, 1955), 34-39.

Robert E. Lee

ROBERT EDWARD LEE, gentleman, scholar, gallant soldier, great general, and true Christian, was born in Westmoreland County, Virginia, on January 19, 1807. He was the youngest son of General Henry Lee, who was familiarly known as "Light-Horse Harry" in the traditions of the war of the Revolution, and who possessed the marked confidence and personal regard of General Washington.[1]

R. E. Lee entered the United States Military Academy in the summer of 1825, after which my acquaintance with him commenced.[2] He was, as I remember him, larger and looked more mature than the average "pleb" [plebe], but less so than Mason,[3] who was destined to be the head of his class. His soldierly bearing and excellent conduct caused him in due succession to rise through the several grades and to be the adjutant of the corps of cadets when he was graduated. It is stated that he had not then a "demerit" mark standing against him, which is quite credible if all "reports" against him had been cancelled, because they were not for wanton or intentional delinquency. Though numerically rated second in his class, his proficiency was such that he was assigned to the engineer corps, which for many years he adorned both as a military and civil engineer.[4]

He was of the highest type of manly beauty, yet seemingly unconscious of it, and so respectful and unassuming as to make him a general favorite before his great powers had an opportunity for manifestation. His mind led him to analytical rather than perceptive methods for obtaining results.

From the date of his graduation in 1829 until 1846 he was engaged in various professional duties, and had by regular promotion attained to the grade of captain of engineers.[5] As such he was assigned to duty with the command of Brigadier-General Wool[6] in the campaign to Chihuahua.[7] Thence the command proceeded to make a junction with General Zachary Taylor[8] in front of Buena Vista. Here Captain Lee was employed in the construction of the defensive work, when General Scott[9] came, armed with discretionary orders, and took Lee for service in the column which Scott was to command,[10] with much else that General Taylor could ill afford to spare. Subsequent events proved that the loss to General Taylor's army was more than compensated by the gain to the general cause.

Avoiding any encroachment upon the domain of history by entering upon a description of campaigns and battles, I cannot forbear from referring to a particular instance of Lee's gallantry and devotion to duty. Before the battle of Contreras,[11] General Scott's troops had become separated by the field of Pedrigal [Pedregal], and it was necessary to communicate instructions to those on the other side of this barrier of rocks and lava. General Scott says in his report that he had sent seven officers since about sundown [of August 19, 1847] to communicate instructions; they had all returned without getting through, "but the gallant and indefatigable Captain Lee, of the engineers, who has been constantly with the operation forces, is just in from Shields [James],[12] Smith [Persifor S.],[13] Cadwallader [Cadwalader, George],"[14] etc. Subsequently General Scott, while giving testimony before a court of inquiry, said: "Captain Lee, engineers, came to me from Contreras with a message from Brigadier-General Smith, I think, about the same time (midnight); he, having passed over the difficult ground by dark—the greatest feat of physical and moral courage performed by any individual, in my knowledge, pending the campaign."

This field of Pedrigal [Pedregal], as described, was impassable on horseback, and crossed with much difficulty by infantry in daylight. After consultation with the generals near to Contreras, it being decided that an attack must be made at daylight, Captain Lee, through storm and darkness, undertook, on foot and alone, to recross the Pedrigal [Pedregal], so as to give General Scott the notice which would insure the cooperation of his divided forces in the morning's attack. This feat was well entitled to the commendation that General Scott bestowed upon it; but the highest praise belongs to Lee's inciting and sustaining motive, *duty*. To bear to the commanding general the needful information, he dared and suffered for that which is the crowning glory of man: he offered himself for the welfare of others.

He went to Mexico with the rank of captain of engineers, and by gallantry and meritorious conduct rose to the rank of colonel in the army, commission by brevet.[15] After his return he resumed his duties as an officer of the Engineer Corps. While employed in the construction of Fort Carroll,[16] near Baltimore, an event occurred which illustrates his nice sentiment of honor. Some members of the Cuban Junta called upon him and offered him the command of an expedition to overthrow the Spanish control of the island. A very large sum of money was to be paid immediately upon his acceptance of their proposition, and a large sum thenceforward was to be paid monthly. Lee came to Washington to converse with me upon the subject.[17] After a brief discussion of the military problem, he said it was not that he had come to consult me about; the question he was considering was whether, while an officer in the United States Army and because of any reputation he might have acquired as such, he could accept a proposition for foreign service against a government with which the United States were at peace.[18] The conclusion was his decision to decline any further correspondence with the Junta.

In 1852 Colonel Lee was made superintendent of the United States Military Academy; a position for which he seemed to be peculiarly fitted as well by his attainment as by his fondness for young people, his fine personal appearance, and impressive manners. When, a year or two thereafter, I visited the academy,[19] and was surprised to see so many gray hairs on his head, he confessed that the cadets did exceedingly worry him, and then it was perceptible that his sympathy with young people was rather an impediment than a qualification for the superintendency.[20]

In 1855 four new regiments were added to the army, two of cavalry and two of infantry.[21] Captain Lee, of the engineers, brevet-colonel of the army, was offered the position of lieutenant-colonel of the Second Regiment of cavalry,[22] which he accepted. He was a bold, graceful horseman, and the son of Light-Horse Harry now seemed to be in his proper element; but the chief of engineers endeavored to persuade him that it was a descent to go from the Engineer Corps into the cavalry.[23] Soon after the regiment was organized and assigned to duty in Texas, the colonel, Albert Sidney Johnston, was selected to command an expedition to Utah,[24] and the command of the regiment and the protection of the frontier of Texas against Indian marauders devolved upon Colonel Lee.[25] There, as in every position he had occupied, diligence, sound judgment, and soldierly endowment made his service successful. In 1859, being on leave of absence in Virginia, he was made available for the suppression of the John Brown raid.[26] As soon as relieved from that special assignment he returned to his command in Texas,[27] and on April 25 [20], 1861, resigned from the United States Army.[28]

Then was his devotion to principle subjected to a crucial test, the severity of which can only be fully realized by a "West Pointer" whose life has been spent in the army. That it was to sever the friendships of youth, to break up the habits of intercourse, of manners, and of thought, others may comprehend and estimate; but the sentiment most profound in the heart of the war-worn cadet, and which made the change most painful to Lee, he has partially expressed in the letters he wrote at the time to his beloved sister and to his venerated friend and commander, General Winfield Scott.[29]

Partisan malignants have not failed to misrepresent the conduct of Lee, even to the extent of charging him with treason and desertion; and, unable to appreciate his sacrifice to the allegiance due to Virginia, they have blindly ascribed his action to selfish ambition.[30] It has been erroneously asserted that he was educated at the expense of the general government, and an attempt has been made thence to deduce a special obligation to adhere to it.

The cadets of the United States Military Academy are apportioned among the States in proportion to the number of representatives they severally have in Congress; that is, one for each congressional district, with ten additional for the country at large. The annual appropriations for the support of the army and navy include the commissioned, warrant, and noncommissioned officers, privates, seamen, etc., etc. The cadets and midshipmen are warrant officers, and while at the academies are receiving elementary instruction in and for the public service. At whose expense are they taught and supported? Surely at that of the people, they who pay the taxes and imposts to supply the treasury with means to meet appropriations as well to pay generals and admirals as cadets and midshipmen. The cadet's obligation for his place and support was to the State, by virtue of whose distributive share he was appointed, and whose contributions supplied the United States treasury; through the State, as a member of the Union, allegiance was due to it, and most usefully and nobly did Lee pay the debt both at home and abroad.[31]

No proposition could be more absurd than that he was prompted by selfish ambition to join the Confederacy. With a small part of his knowledge of the relative amount of material of war possessed by the North and South, any one must have seen that the chances of war were against us; but if thrice-armed Justice should enable the South to maintain her independence, as our fathers had done, notwithstanding the unequal contest, what selfish advantage could it bring to Lee? If, as some among us yet expected, many hoped, and all wished, there should be a peaceful separation, he would have left behind him all he had gained by long and brilliant service, and could not have in our small army greater rank than was proffered to him in the larger one he had left. If active hostilities were prosecuted, his large property would be so exposed as to incur serious injury, if not destruction. His mother, Virginia, had revoked the grants she had voluntarily made to the Federal Government, and asserted the state sovereignty and independence she had won from the mother-country by the war of the Revolution; and thus, it was regarded, the allegiance of her sons became wholly her own. Above the voice of his friends at Washington, advising and entreating him to stay with them, rose the cry of Virginia calling her sons to defend her against threatened invasion. Lee heeded this cry only; alone he rode forth, as he had crossed the Pedrigal [Pedregal], his guiding star being duty, and offered his sword to Virginia. His offer was accepted, and he was appointed to the chief command of the forces of the State.[32] Though his reception was most flattering and the confidence manifested in him unlimited, his conduct was conspicuous for the modesty which had always been characteristic of him.

The South had been involved in war without having made due preparation for it. She was without a navy, without even a merchant marine commensurate with her wants during peace; without arsenals, armories, foundries, manufactories, or stores on hand to supply those wants. Lee exerted himself to the utmost to raise and organize troops in Virginia, and when the State joined the Confederacy he was invited to come to Montgomery and explain the condition of his command; but his engagements were so pressing that he sent his second officer, General Joseph E. Johnston,[33] to furnish the desired information.

When the capital of the Confederacy was removed from Montgomery to Richmond [May 29, 1861], Lee, under orders of the President, was charged with the general direction of army affairs. In this position the same pleasant relations which had always existed between them continued, and Lee's indefatigable attention to the details of the various commands was of much benefit to the public service. In the meantime disasters, confusion, and disagreement among the commands in western Virginia made it necessary to send there an officer of higher rank than any then on duty in that section. The service was disagreeable, toilsome, and in no wise promising to give distinction to a commander. Passing by all reference to others, suffice it to say that at last Lee was asked to go, and, not counting the cost, he unhesitatingly prepared to start. By concentrating the troops, and by a judicious selection of the position, he compelled the enemy finally to retreat.[34]

There is an incident in this campaign which has never been reported, save as it was orally given to me by General Lee, with a request that I should take no official notice of it. A strong division [J. J. Reynolds' Brigade] of the enemy was reported to be encamped in a valley [Tygart's] which, one of the colonels [Albert Rust] said he had found by reconnaissance, could readily be approached on one side, and he proposed, with his regiment [3rd Arkansas Infantry], to surprise and attack. General Lee accepted his proposition, but told him that he himself would, in the meantime, with several regiments, ascend the mountain [Cheat] that overlooked the valley on the other side; and at dawn of day on a morning fixed the colonel was to make his assault. His firing was to be the signal for a joint attack from three directions. During the night Lee made a toilsome ascent of the mountain and was in position at the time agreed upon. The valley was covered by a dense fog. Not hearing the signal, he went by a winding path down the side of the mountain and saw the enemy preparing breakfast and otherwise so engaged as to indicate that they were entirely ignorant of any danger. Lee returned to his own command, told them what he had seen, and, though the expected signal had not been given by which the attacking regiment and another detachment were to engage in the assault, he proposed that the regiments then with him should surprise the camp, which he believed, under the circumstances, might successfully be done. The colonels went to consult their men and returned to inform him that they were cold, wet, and hungry as to be unfit for the enterprise. The fog was then lifting, and it was necessary to attack immediately or to withdraw before being discovered by the much larger force in the valley. Lee therefore withdrew his small command and safely conducted them to his encampment.

The colonel [Rust] who was to give the signal for the joint attack, misapprehending the purpose, reported that when he arrived upon the ground he found the encampment protected by a heavy abatis,[35] which prevented him from making a sudden charge, as he had expected, not understanding that if he had fired his guns at any distance he would have secured the joint attack of the other detachments, and probably brought about an entire victory. Lee generously forbore to exonerate himself when the newspapers in Richmond criticized him severely, one denying him any other consideration except that which he enjoyed as "the President's pet."[36]

It was an embarrassment to the Executive to be deprived of the advice of General Lee, but it was deemed necessary again to detach him to look after affairs on the coast of Carolina and Georgia,[37] and so violent had been the unmerited attacks upon him by the Richmond press that it was thought proper to give him a letter to the Governor of South Carolina, stating what manner of man had been sent to him.[38] There his skill as an engineer was manifested in the defences he constructed and devised. On his return to Richmond he resumed his functions of general supervisor of military affairs.

In the spring of 1862 Bishop Meade lay dangerously ill. This venerable ecclesiastic had taught General Lee his catechism when a boy,[39] and when he was announced to the bishop the latter asked to have him shown in immediately. He answered Lee's inquiry as to how he felt by saying, "Nearly gone, but I wished to see you once more," and then in a feeble voice added: "God bless you, Robert, and fit you for your high and responsible duties!" The great soldier stood reverently by the bed of his early preceptor in Christianity, but the saintly patriot saw beyond the hero the pious boy to whom he had taught the catechism; first he gave his dying blessing to Robert, and then, struggling against exhaustion, invoked Heaven's guidance for the general.[40]

After the battle of Seven Pines Lee was assigned to the command of the Army of Virginia.[41] Thus far his duties had been of a kind to confer a great benefit, but to be unseen and unappreciated by the public.[42] Now he had an opportunity for the employment of his remarkable power of generalization while attending to the minutest details. The public saw manifestation of the first, but could not estimate the extent to which the great results achieved were due to the exact order, systematic economy, and regularity begotten of his personal attention to the proper adjustment of even the smallest part of that mighty machine, a well-organized, disciplined army. His early instructor, in a published letter, seemed to regard the boy's labor of finishing a drawing on a slate as an excess of care.[43] Was it so? No doubt, so far as the particular task was concerned; but this seedling is to be judged by the fruit the tree bore. That little drawing on the slate was the prototype of the exact investigations which crowned with success his labors as a civil and military engineer as well as a commander of armies. May it not have been, not only by endowment but also from these early efforts, that his mind became so rounded, systematic, and complete that his notes written on the battle-field and in the saddle had the precision of form and lucidity of expression found in those written in the quiet of his tent? These incidents are related, not because of their intrinsic importance, but as presenting an example for the emulation of youths whose admiration of Lee may induce them to follow the toilsome methods by which he attained to true greatness and enduring fame.

In the early days of June, 1862, General McClellan threatened the capital, Richmond, with an army numerically much superior to that to the command of which Lee had been assigned.[44] A day or two after he had joined [taken command of] the army, I was riding to the front and saw a number of horses hitched in front of a house, and among them recognized General Lee's. Upon dismounting and going in, I found some general officers engaged in consultation with him as to how McClellan's advance could be checked,[45] and one of them commenced to explain the disparity of force and with pencil and paper to show how the enemy could throw out his boyaus,[46] and by successive parallels make his approach irresistible. "Stop, stop," said Lee;

"if you go to ciphering we are whipped beforehand."[47] He ordered the construction of earthworks, put guns in position for a defensive line on the south side of the Chickahominy,[48] and then commenced the strategic movement which was the inception of the seven-days' battles, ending in uncovering the capital and driving the enemy to the cover of his gunboats in the James River.[49]

There never was a greater mistake than that which has attributed to General Lee what General Charles Lee in his reply to General Washington called the "rascally virtue." I have had occasion to remonstrate with General Lee for exposing himself, as I thought, unnecessarily in reconnaissance, but he justified himself by saying he "could not understand things so well unless he saw them." In the excitement of battle his natural combativeness would sometimes overcome his habitual self-control; thus it twice occurred in the campaign against Grant that the men seized his bridle to restrain him from his purpose to lead them in a charge."[50]

He was always careful not to wound the sensibilities of any one, and sometimes, with an exterior jest or compliment, would give what, if properly appreciated, was instruction for the better performance of some duty; for example, if he thought a general officer was not visiting his command as early and as often as was desirable, he might admire his horse and suggest that the animal would be improved by more exercise.

He was not of the grave, formal nature that he seemed to some who only knew him when sad realities cast dark shadows upon him; but even then the humor natural to him would occasionally break out. For instance, General Lee called at my office for a ride to the defences of Richmond, then under construction. He was mounted on a stallion which some kind friend had recently sent him.[51] As I mounted my horse, his was restive and kicked at mine. We rode on quietly together, though Lee was watchful to keep his horse in order. Passing by an encampment, we saw near a tent two stallions tied at a safe distance from one another. "There," said he, "is a man worse off than I am." When asked to explain, he said: "Don't you see he has two stallions? I have but one."

His habits had always been rigidly temperate, and his fare in camp was of the simplest.[52] I remember on one battle-field riding past where he and his staff were taking their luncheon.

He invited me to share it, and when I dismounted for the purpose it proved to have consisted only of bacon and cornbread. The bacon had all been eaten, and there were only some crusts of cornbread left, which, however, having been saturated with the bacon gravy, were in those hard times altogether acceptable, as General Lee was assured in order to silence his regrets.

While he was on duty in South Carolina and Georgia, Lee's youngest son, Robert,[53] then a mere boy, left school and came down to Richmond, announcing his purpose to go into the army. His older brother, Custis,[54] was a member of my staff, and, after a conference, we agreed that it was useless to send the boy back to school, and that he probably would not wait in Richmond for the return of his father; so we selected a battery which had been organized in Richmond and sent Robert to join it.[55] General Lee told me that at the battle of Sharpsburg this battery suffered so much that it had to be withdrawn for repairs and some fresh horses;[56] but, as he had no troops even to form a reserve, as soon as the battery could be made useful it was ordered forward. He said that as it passed him a boy mounted as a driver of one of the guns, much stained with powder, said, "Are you going to put us in again, general?" After replying to him in the affirmative, he was struck by the voice of the boy and asked him, "Whose son are you?" to which he answered, "I am Robbie," whereupon his father said, "God bless you, my son, you must go in."

When General Lee was in camp near Richmond his friends frequently sent him something to improve his mess-table. A lady noted for the very good bread she made had frequently favored him with some. One day, as we were riding through the street, she was standing in her front door and bowed to us. The salutation was, of course, returned. After we had passed he asked me who she was. I told him she was the lady who sent him such good bread. He was very sorry he had not known it, but to go back would prove that he had not recognized her as he should have done. His habitual avoidance of any seeming harshness, which caused him sometimes, instead of giving a command, to make a suggestion, was probably a defect.[57] I believe that he had in this manner indicated that supplies were to be deposited for him at Amelia Court-House, but the testimony of General Breckenridge [Breckinridge],[58] Secretary of War, of General St. John,[59] Commissary General, and

Louis Harvey [Harvie],[60] president of the Richmond and Danville Railroad,[61] conclusively proves that no such requisition was made upon either of the persons who should have received it; and, further, that there were supplies both at Danville and Richmond which could have been sent to Amelia Court-House if information had been received that they were wanted there.[62]

Much has been written in regard to the failure to occupy the Round Top at Gettysburg early in the morning of the second day's battle, to which failure the best judgment attributes our want of entire success in that battle. Whether this was due to the order not being sufficiently positive or not, I will leave to the historians who are discussing that important event.[63] I have said that Lee's natural temper was combative, and to this may be ascribed his attack on the third day at Gettysburg, when the opportunity had not been seized which his genius saw was the gate to victory.[64] It was this last attack to which I have thought he referred when he said it was all his fault, thereby sparing others from whatever blame was due for what had previously occurred.[65]

After the close of the war, while I was in prison and Lee was on parole,[66] we were both indicted on a charge of treason; but, in hot haste to get in their work, the indictment was drawn with the fatal omission of an overt act. General Grant interposed in the case of General Lee, on the ground that he had taken his parole and that he was, therefore, not subject to arrest.[67] Another grand jury was summoned, and a bill was presented against me alone, and amended by inserting specifications of overt acts. General Lee was summoned as a witness before that grand jury, the object being to prove by him that I was responsible for certain things done by him during the war. I was in Richmond, having been released by virtue of the writ of habeas corpus. General Lee met me very soon after having given his testimony before the grand jury, and told me that to the inquiry whether he had not, in the specified cases, acted upon my orders, he said that he had always consulted me when he had the opportunity, both on the field and elsewhere; that after discussion, if not before, we had always agreed, and therefore he had done with my consent and approval only what he might have done if he had not consulted me, and that he accepted the full responsibility for his acts. He said he had endeavored to present the matter as distinctly as he could, and looked up to see what effect he was producing upon the grand jury. Immediately before him sat a big black negro [Negro], whose head had fallen back on the rail of the bench he sat on; his mouth was wide open, and he was fast asleep. General Lee pleasantly added that, if he had had any vanity as an orator, it would have received a rude check.

The evident purpose was to offer to Lee a chance to escape by transferring to me the responsibility for overt acts. Not only to repel the suggestion, but unequivocally to avow his individual responsibility, with all that, under existing circumstances, was implied in this, was the highest reach of moral courage and gentlemanly pride. Those circumstances were exceptionally perilous to him. He had been indicted for treason; the United States President had vindictively threatened to make treason odious; the dregs of society had been thrown to the surface; judicial seats were held by political adventurers; the United States judge of the Virginia district had answered to a committee of Congress that he could pack a jury so as to convict Davis or Lee,— and it was under such surroundings that he met the grand jury and testified as stated above. Arbitrary power might pervert justice and trample on right, but could not turn the knightly Lee from the path of honor and truth.

Descended from a long line of illustrious warriors and statesmen, Robert Edward Lee added new glory to the name he bore, and, whether measured by a martial or an intellectual standard, will compare favorably with those whose reputation it devolved upon him to sustain and emulate.

JEFFERSON DAVIS

A
PORTFOLIO
OF
SELECTED PHOTOGRAPHS
OF
ROBERT E. LEE

This is thought to be the first photograph of Robert E. Lee. The boy with him is probably William Henry Fitzhugh "Rooney" Lee, his second son. The date of the daguerreotype is given as late 1845. It may have been taken at Brady's New York Studio. Lee was thirty-eight at the time and Rooney was eight.

First fully authenticated photograph of Lee. It is another daguerreotype and was probably taken in the spring of 1846. It shows Lee in the uniform of a captain of engineers and how he appeared in the Mexican War. Lee's side whiskers have been replaced by a moustache. His famous signature appears in the right-hand corner.

A daguerreotype by Brady taken in either 1850 or 1851. Lee was a brevet colonel at the time of this photograph and was in charge of the construction of Fort Carroll near Baltimore.

This is thought to be the only photograph of General Lee taken in the field. It probably is the work of Minnis & Cowell of Richmond. Note that the moustache has been replaced by a beard and Lee now parts his hair on the right side. The date of this fine photograph is probably the spring of 1862.

Here, the reader sees the Commander of the Army of
Northern Virginia at the height of his success. This photo-
graph was taken by Minnis & Cowell of Richmond either in late
February or early March, 1863. It is the first formally posed
photograph of Lee. He is fifty-six years old—his victory at
Chancellersville is still two months away.

The famous left full profile photograph taken by J. Vannerson of Richmond, in early 1864. It is one of a series of four photographs taken by the famous Richmond photographer for Edward V. Valentine, the Virginia sculptor. This photograph and the other three were used by Valentine to make a statuette of Lee to be sold in European bazaars for a Confederate fund-raising drive.

Lee is supposed to have liked this photograph the best of any taken. It is the work of J. W. Davis, a Richmond photographer and was taken in the spring or summer of 1864. The General has started to trim his beard shorter and the lump on his right cheek bone is clearly discernable.

Here appears for the first time before a photographer's lense Lee riding his famous gray mount, "Traveller." The time is probably late October or early November, 1864, at Petersburg. The photographer is unknown.

Brady took this photograph of Lee (after some persuasion) on April 16, 1865, the day after Lee returned from Appomattox. The picture was taken on the lower back porch of Lee's Franklin Street house in Richmond. The General is wearing the same new uniform that he wore when surrendering to Grant, minus the sword, boots and gauntlets.

Another picture by Brady, taken at the same place and time as the preceding photograph. General Lee is flanked on his right by his eldest son, Major General George Washington Custis Lee. On Lee's left stands his assistant adjutant general, Colonel Walter Taylor.

Left full profile of Lee taken by Brady on April 16, 1865. Probably these three photographs by Brady have been copied, published and reproduced more than any other photographs of the great Southern leader.

This study of Lee on Traveller was taken by Photographer Miley of Lexington, Virginia during September, 1866. At the time General Lee was president of Washington College at Lexington. Traveller outlived Lee only a few months, dying of lockjaw in June, 1871. Traveller's bones were preserved, cleaned and mounted, and can be seen today in the Confederate Museum in Richmond.

On a trip to Baltimore from Lexington in the spring of 1869 Lee stopped in Washington to see President Grant. While in the capitol he stopped at Brady's Studio and this is one of the photographs that his friend Brady took. Many Lee scholars consider this to be the best post-war photograph of the General.

Robert E. Lee seldom was photographed from the right side. This is one of two photographs in existence which shows Lee's right profile sharply defined. Some Lee scholars believe this to be the last photograph taken of Lee. It was taken by Boude and Miley in Lexington, probably in the spring of 1870. The lump on Lee's right cheekbone is clearly visible.

Two great Virginians, Robert E. Lee and Joseph E. Johnston, had their photograph taken together by D. J. Ryan of Savannah, Georgia in early April, 1870. Both men were sixty-three at the time. They were graduated together from West Point in 1829 and were lifelong friends. This is probably the last picture taken of Robert E. Lee. He would be dead within a few months. Johnston lived until 1891.

The death mask of Robert E. Lee. It was made the day that he died, October 12, 1870. The original plaster cast is in the Confederate Museum at Richmond.

Notes
and
References

¹Henry Lee, familiarly known as "Light-Horse Harry" Lee, was born at "Leesylvania" near Dumfries, Virginia in 1756. He was graduated from the College of New Jersey (later Princeton University) in 1773 and was preparing to go to England to study law when the Revolutionary War broke out.

In 1776 young Lee was appointed a captain in Theodorick Bland's regiment of Virginia cavalry. He attracted General George Washington's attention early in the war with his gallantry as a scout and raider. In 1778 Lee was promoted to major and given command of a mixed battalion of light-horse and infantry known as "Lee's Legion." From this command came his famous nickname, "Light-Horse Harry." Lee's greatest exploit in the northern theater of operations was his surprise of the British outpost at Paulus Hook, New Jersey on August 19, 1779. For this victory, Major Lee received a gold medal, the thanks of Congress, and the praise of General Washington, who regarded the young Virginian almost as a son. Light-Horse Harry was promoted to lieutenant colonel in 1780 and sent to the southern theater of operations to assist General Nathaniel Greene, who was in need of a daring cavalry commander. Lee fought gallantly at both Guiliford Court House (March 15, 1781) and Eutaw Springs (September 8, 1781) and bested the famous British cavalry commander, Colonel Banastre Tarleton, on the several occasions when their forces met. Lee was present at the siege of Yorktown and witnessed the surrender of Cornwallis on October 19, 1781.

Following the war and until 1801 Light-Horse Harry Lee had a successful military and political career. He was sent to the Continental Congress from Virginia in 1785 and was an active member (a Federalist) of the Virginia convention that ratified the United States Constitution in 1788. He was the governor of Virginia from 1792 to 1795. In 1799 Lee was elected to the National House of Representatives. It was Henry Lee, who in a resolution to Congress on the death of Washington (December 14, 1799), referred to the great wartime commander as "first in war, first in peace, first in the hearts of his countrymen." While serving as governor of Virginia, President

Washington appointed Lee commander of the army that suppressed the Whiskey Rebellion in Western Pennsylvania in 1794. This was accomplished without bloodshed and enhanced Light-Horse Harry's military stature and his standing with Washington. Lee served as a temporary major-general in the American Army during the emergency created by the undeclared war with France in 1798-99.

Following his lone term in Congress, Lee drifted into financial misfortune and political obscurity. He was imprisoned twice for indebtedness and was pummeled and almost fatally stabbed by a mob in Baltimore while protecting an editor who dared to oppose the War of 1812. Burdened by debts brought on by unwise speculation in western lands and smarting under public criticism for his opposition to the War of 1812, Henry Lee left Virginia in the summer of 1813 for the Barbados Islands. While returning to Virginia in the spring of 1818, he was mortally stricken on board ship and was put ashore at Dungeness, Cumberland Island, Georgia. Although tenderly cared for by the daughter of his old commander, Nathaniel Greene, Henry Lee died on March 25 and was buried on the island. In 1913 the remains of Henry Lee, one of the first great American cavalrymen, were removed to the Lee Chapel of Washington and Lee University, where his famous son was buried.

In 1812 Henry Lee published his *Memoirs of the War in the Southern Department*. It was re-issued in 1827. General Lee, in 1869, published the third edition of his father's work and added to it a short (sixty-eight page) biography of Henry Lee. This was the longest single composition ever written by the Confederate commander. While Robert E. Lee's letters were free flowing, smooth, and warm, his few efforts of formal writing were dull and ponderous.

(Douglas Southall Freeman, *R. E. Lee* (4 vols.; New York: Charles Scribner's Sons, 1934), I, 2-33; IV, 415-19. *Dictionary of American Biography*, Dumas Malone (ed.), (11 vols.; New York: Charles Scribner's Sons, 1961), VI, 107-08.)

[2]Jefferson Davis was appointed a cadet at the United States Military Academy at West Point from the state of Mississippi on September 1, 1824. He was graduated number twenty-three in a class of thirty-three on July 1, 1828. Davis was the 530th man to be graduated from the Military Academy. His class

standings while he was a cadet were not impressive. At the end of his fourth class year (freshman) he stood thirty-second in a class of forty-eight. At the end of his third class year (sophomore) his standing was number twenty-nine in a class of thirty-nine members. Davis finished his second class year (junior) number twenty-nine in a class of thirty-seven.

Inasmuch as Robert E. Lee entered West Point the year after Jefferson Davis and the entire Corps of Cadets numbered not more than 250 at that time, the two probably knew each other well during their three years together at the Academy.

(Letter to the editor from Kenneth W. Rapp, Assistant Archivist, USMA, dated 20 May, 1966. Register of Graduates, *op. cit.*, 123.)

[3]Charles Mason was born in Pompey, Onondaga County, New York, on October 24, 1804. He was graduated from the United States Military Academy at West Point number one in the class of 1829. Mason was the 541st man to be graduated from the Academy. He was commissioned a brevet second lieutenant in the corps of engineers upon graduating and remained at West Point as an assistant professor of engineering. Charles Mason resigned his commission on December 31, 1831, to study law.

Mason was admitted to the New York bar in June, 1832. He went west in 1836 and was appointed Chief Justice of the Supreme Court of the Territory of Iowa when that trans-Mississippi area was organized as a territory in 1838. After Iowa became a state in December, 1846, Mason settled in Des Moines as an attorney. In 1851 he was elected county judge of Des Moines County and became instrumental in codifying the laws of the state. He was appointed by President Pierce as the Federal Commissioner of Patents, a position from which he resigned in 1857 to become a member of the first Iowa State Board of Education. Just prior to the Civil War, Charles Mason returned to Washington to practice patent law.

The number one scholar of the Class of 1829 did not fight in the Civil War. Politically a Democrat, he was defeated for a position on the Supreme Court of Iowa in 1863 and for governor of the state in 1867. Mason served as a delegate from Iowa to the Democrat nominating conventions of 1868 and 1872. Drawing upon his West Point education and teaching experience he wrote much in the field of drainage and sanitation. The last years of his life were spent practicing law. He maintained offices in both Washington and Iowa. Charles Mason died in Iowa on February 27, 1882.

(Register of Gradutes, *op. cit.*, 124. Freeman, *op. cit.*, 1, 83. Francis B. Heitman, *Historical Register and Dictionary of the United States Army*, (2 vols.; Washington: Government Printing Office, 1903), I, 694.)

[4]Robert E. Lee was appointed to the United States Military Academy at West Point at the age of nineteen years, four months by the famous South Carolina senator, John C. Calhoun. (By coincidence, Jefferson Davis had also been appointed to the Military Academy by Calhoun the year before Lee.)

Cadet Lee's performance at West Point was outstanding; his awards and honors have been equalled by few cadets before or since. He was designated a "Distinguished Cadet" at the end of each academic year and at his graduation July 1, 1829. (The term "Distinguished Cadet" was awarded only to the first five cadets in relative class academic standing.) As a third classman (sophomore) he served as a staff sergeant, a cadet rank usually reserved for second classmen (juniors). During both his third and second class years, Lee was appointed an acting assistant professor of mathematics. Acting assistant professorships were normally filled by first classmen (seniors). The most coveted and important cadet rank at West Point was that of Corps Adjutant. The Corps Adjutant was selected by the superintendent of the Academy from among the first classmen who were outstanding scholars, had the finest military bearing, and had the best record on the drill grounds. Robert E. Lee was selected to fill this key position.

Other fine achievements attained by Lee during his four years at the United States Military Academy included perfect scores in his final exams (as a first classman) in both artillery and tactics. He was one of the few cadets to be graduated without a demerit and earned the honor of ranking second in a class of forty-six.

The class leaders at West Point were awarded the privilege of selecting the branch of service in which they wished to be commissioned. Most class leaders, like Lee, requested assignment to the corps of engineers. The branches of the service generally were filled in the following order: corps of engineers, artillery, cavalry, and infantry. Lee was commissioned a brevet second lieutenant in the corps of engineers on July 1, 1829.

(Freeman, *op. cit.*, I, 61-82. Letter to the editor from Kenneth W. Rapp, Archivist, United States Military Academy, dated 7 December, 1965.)

[5]Robert E. Lee's assignments during the period of time from graduation (1829) to 1846 were primarily concerned with engineering assignments in the field. His first post-graduation duty (1829-31) was working on fortifications under the supervision of Major Samuel Babcock at Cockspur Island near Savannah, Georgia. In May, 1831, Lee was transferred to Old Point Comfort at Hampton Roads, Virginia, to assist in completing Forts Monroe and Calhoun. It was while he was assigned at Old Point Comfort that Lee received word of his promotion from brevet rank to regular second lieutenant in 1832. In November, 1834, the young Virginian was transferred to Washington as an assistant to the Chief of Engineers, Brigadier General Charles I. Gratiot. While assigned in Washington in the spring and summer of 1835, Lee was sent to the Great Lakes area to survey the long disputed boundary between Michigan and Ohio. The dispute was of long standing and had reached the stage of almost provoking an armed clash between the two states. While Lee was assigned to Gratiot's office he was promoted to first lieutenant—his commission to date from November 21, 1836.

Robert E. Lee's greatest challenge in the field of engineering awaited him at St. Louis, where he was ordered to report in April, 1837. The Mississippi River's ever-changing channel was threatening to reduce the busy port of St. Louis to a mud flat. After four years of intermittent work, Engineer Lee succeeded in diverting the main river channel to the western bank and saved the port from oblivion. After this feat the Virginian was recognized as one of the most brilliant young civil engineers in the United States. While assigned to the St. Louis project on August 7, 1838, Lee was promoted to captain of engineers. He had served as a first lieutenant less than two years; his next promotions would come much slower.

In October of 1840, Lee was assigned to duty inspecting fortifications along the East Coast, particularly those forts in the Carolinas and in New York Harbor. After inspecting Fort Macon near Beaufort, South Carolina, and Fort Caswell at the mouth of Cape Fear River in North Carolina, Lee journeyed to New York, where he was to remain until the Mexican War. Captain Lee and his family resided at Fort Hamilton while he supervised the rebuilding and repairing of the series of forts guarding New York City. During his sojourn at Fort Hamilton, Lee was assigned on temporary duty elsewhere on two different occasions. In June, 1844 he was named by President Tyler to a special commission (which replaced the Board of Visitors) to assist in examining the graduating cadets at West Point. Here, for the first time, Lee was closely associated with the commander in chief of the army, General Winfield Scott, who was also a member of the commission. This association turned out to be one of the major events in Lee's life. In December of the same year the captain of engineers was assigned on temporary duty for the winter (1844-45) as the office assistant to the Chief of Engineers (Colonel Joseph G. Totten) at Washington.

Lee reported back to Fort Hamilton in the spring of 1845 to continue his work in strengthening the defense complex of New York Harbor. In September he was appointed a member of the Board of Engineers for the Atlantic Coast Defense with his duty station remaining at Fort Hamilton. Lee remained here until August 19, 1846, when he was ordered to report to Brigadier General John E. Wool for service in the Mexican War.

(Freeman, *op. cit.*, I, 94-202.)

[6]John Ellis Wool was born at Newburgh, New York, on February 29, 1784. Upon the outbreak of the War of 1812, Wool raised a company at Troy, New York, was commissioned a captain in the 13th U. S. Infantry Regiment, and distinguished himself at Queenstown Heights (October 13, 1812), where he was badly wounded, and at Plattsburg (September 11, 1814). He was brevetted a lieutenant colonel for gallant conduct at Plattsburg.

On April 29, 1816, Wool was promoted to colonel and assigned as inspector general of the army. He was promoted to brigadier general in 1841.

At the outbreak of the Mexican War, General Wool commanded the "Army of the Center," whose objective it was to capture Chihuahua City (State of Chihuahua, Mexico). This objective was not realized; for soon after he had crossed the

Rio Grande, he was ordered to join General Zachary Taylor's Army near Monterrey. Wool was second in command to Taylor at the Battle of Buena Vista (February 22-23, 1847), where he was brevetted major general for meritorious service. Several years later Congress voted him a sword and thanks for his efforts at Buena Vista.

Wool was commanding the Department of the East when Fort Sumter was fired on in April, 1861. He was transferred to Virginia in the summer of 1861 and was successful in keeping Fortress Monroe from Confederate hands. The septuagenarian veteran of three wars was promoted to major general in the regular army on May 16, 1862. Thus he became the fourth ranking general in the Federal Army, following McClellan, Fremont, and Halleck in that order. In the summer of 1862, Wool commanded both the Middle Department and the 8th Corps. The oldest officer on either side to exercise active command in the Civil War, he was retired because of his age in July, 1863.

Following the war General Wool resided at Troy, New York, where he died on November 10, 1869, at age eighty-five.

(Mark M. Boatner III, *The Civil War Dictionary*, (New York: David McKay Company, Inc., 1959), 948. Ezra J. Warner, *Generals in Blue*, (Baton Rouge: Louisiana State University Press, 1964), 573-74. *Dictionary of American Biography, op. cit.*, X, 513-14).

[7]According to War Department plans, the American Army was to launch a three-pronged drive to capture the northern provinces or states of Mexico. General Stephen W. Kearney's "Army of the West" was to advance west from Fort Leavenworth to California via Santa Fe. General Zachary Taylor's "Army of Observation" was to strike south across the Rio Grande toward Monterrey and Saltillo. General John E. Wool's "Army of the Center" was to march southwest from San Antonio, cross the Rio Grande, and capture Chihuahua City.

Captain Lee joined Wool's army at San Antonio, point of concentration for the Army of the Center, on September 21, 1846. San Antonio, normally a sleepy border town of some 2,000 inhabitants (mostly Mexicans) was a bustling military camp of 3,500 soldiers, 350 wagons, and eight artillery pieces in late September, 1846.

On September 28 the advanced column of Wool's Army

moved out toward the Rio Grande. Lee shared engineering duties with Captain William D. Fraser, a West Point graduate (Class of 1834) who had arrived at San Antonio prior to the Virginian. After twenty-one years of military service and nearly forty years old, Robert E. Lee experienced his first duty with troops on a march against the enemy. It would be far from his last!

Crossing the Rio Grande near the small Mexican town of Presidio Rio Grande called for an engineering feat of major proportions. At this point the river was 300 yards wide, more than four feet deep, and swift flowing. A "flying bridge," constructed of pontoons and framed timbers in four days under the direction of engineers Fraser and Lee, enabled the Army of the Center "with all of its wheeled and animal transport to cross dry shod." Besides bridging streams, the two engineering officers were kept busy supervising the clearing of obstacles from the line of march, preparing roads, and building earthworks at bridgeheads and points of temporary concentration.

Wool's army advanced into Mexico as far south as Monclova (a town of 8,000 and former capitol of the Mexican states of Coahuila and Tejas). Here it halted on October 20, 1846, awaiting news and orders from Taylor's Army to the east with which it had been ordered to cooperate. During the march to Monclova, Captain Fraser had returned to San Antonio, leaving Lee as the sole engineering officer with Wool's Army.

In late November, General Taylor ordered Wool to move from Monclova to Parras, where he could more easily follow one of three courses of action: join Taylor at Monterrey, join General William J. Worth at Saltillo (the advanced element of Taylor's command), or move northwest and invest Chihuahua City. On December 17, Taylor ordered Wool to reinforce Worth at Saltillo, as General Antonio López de Santa Anna, the self-styled "Napoleon of the West," was reported to be moving on that city with an army of 20,000. Wool joined Worth's command near Saltillo (at Encontada) just before Christmas, 1846. The rumor concerning Santa Anna's advance proved to be false; and the combined armies, comprising some 6,000 troops, went into a defensive posture. While at Encantada, General Wool assigned Lee the additional duty of acting inspector general.

Although "Granny" Wool was a strict disciplinarian and provoked controversies with several of his senior subordinate commanders, he was an experienced leader and able organizer. The Army of the Center under his leadership had performed remarkably well. It had marched 900 miles over deserts and mountains in less than two months marching time with 3,000 men; eight pieces of artillery; 350 wagons laden with sixty days' provisions; 400,000 rounds of small-arms ammunition; and 200 rounds for the artillery without the loss of a man, a horse, a wagon, or a cartridge. Few commanders in the American Army (or any other army) could claim the same.

(Freeman, *op. cit.*, I, 203-17. Robert Selph Henry, *The Mexican War*, (Indianapolis: Bobbs, Merrill Co., 1950), 181-83. Alfred Hoyt Bill, *Rehearsal For Conflict*, (New York: Alfred A. Knopf, 1947), 191-92. Oliver L. Spaulding, *The United States Army in Peace and War*, (New York: G. P. Putnam's Sons, 1937), 189-200.)

[8]Zachary Taylor, known as "Old Rough and Ready," was born at Montebello, Orange County, Virginia, on November 24, 1784.

In 1808 he was appointed a first lieutenant in the 7th Infantry Regiment. In 1810 he was promoted to captain, and the following year by orders of General William Henry Harrison (governor of the Indiana Territory) was assigned command of Fort Knox in Kentucky.

During the War of 1812, Taylor fought Indians along the western frontier and was brevetted major for distinguished service.

In the decade and a half following the War of 1812, Taylor served in several infantry regiments: the 3rd, the 4th, and finally the 1st. He built Fort Jessup on the Louisiana frontier in 1822, served as recruiting officer at Louisville in 1824, was a member of various boards, and acted as the Indian superintendent at Fort Snelling (Minnesota Territory) from 1829 to 1832.

On April 4, 1832, at the age of forty-seven, Taylor was promoted to colonel and given command of the 1st U. S. Infantry Regiment. He fought with distinction in two conflicts: the Blackhawk War (1832-33) and the Seminole War (1836-42). In the former conflict Taylor turned over the captured Chief Blackhawk to young Lieutenant Jefferson Davis for custody and escort back to Jefferson Barracks. The same Jefferson Davis who would soon elope with Taylor's daughter and later become President of the Southern Confederacy. In the latter war Old Rough and Ready severely defeated the Indians at the Battle of

Okeechobee (Christmas day, 1837), for which achievement he was brevetted brigadier general.

In May, 1844, General Taylor was ordered to Fort Jessup in anticipation of the annexation of Texas and possible trouble with Mexico. In the summer of 1845 he advanced with an army of about 4,500 men to Corpus Christi at the mouth of the Nueces River in Texas. The following January Taylor was ordered to advance to the Rio Grande. The Mexican Army crossed over the Rio Grande in May, 1846, and Taylor decisively defeated General Arista's much larger Mexican force at Palo Alto (May 8) and at Resaca de la Palma (May 9). Zachary Taylor was promoted immediately to major general by brevet and his army designated as the Army of the Rio Grande. During September, 1846, with an army of 6,000 (split equally between regulars and volunteers), General Taylor attacked the key city of northern Mexico, Monterrey, and after a three-day battle (September 21-24, 1846) at the point of the bayonet, forced the city to capitulate. Advancing southward from Monterrey, he met a vastly superior Mexican army under Santa Anna and defeated it after a bloody two-day battle (February 22-23, 1847) at Buena Vista.

Buena Vista was the last major battle fought in the northern provinces of Mexico. Most of Taylor's force was transferred to Winfield Scott's Army which was assembling at Brazos Santiago for the drive on Mexico City via Vera Cruz. Taylor remained in northern Mexico until the fall of 1847, when he returned to his Louisiana plantation, Cypress Grove, to receive the plaudits of the public and be hailed the "Hero of Buena Vista."

Taylor was drafted for president by the Whig party in 1848 and was elected the twelfth President of the United States later that year. He served only a little over a year in office, dying on July 9, 1850 from the effects of a heat stroke.

(*Dictionary of American Biography,* op. cit., IX, 349-354.)

[9]Winfield Scott, known as "Old Fuss and Feathers," and the only American of the nineteenth century to serve as a general officer in three major wars, was born near Petersburg, Virginia, on June 13, 1786.

Scott was a physical giant, at nineteen he stood six feet five inches and weighed 230 pounds. He was educated by private tutors but did attend the College of William and Mary for a short while. Young Scott studied law at Petersburg, but the military service held a great attraction for him. During the year 1807 he joined the Petersburg Troop of Cavalry. In 1808 Scott was commissioned a captain of artillery in the regular army and recruited a company in Petersburg and Richmond. During the winter of 1811-12 he served on Brigadier General Wade Hampton's staff in New Orleans.

At the start of the War of 1812, Scott was promoted to lieutenant colonel and recruited his own regiment at Philadelphia. He played a heroic part at the Battle of Queenstown Heights (October 13, 1812), where he was captured but paroled the following month. Scott was promoted to colonel during March, 1813, and to brigadier general in the regular army on March 9, 1814. In the spring of 1814 he was given command of a brigade which he trained to a fine edge and which bore the brunt of the fighting at Chippewa (July 4-5, 1814) and at Lundy's Lane (July 25, 1814). Scott was badly wounded in the latter battle after having two horses shot from under him. In a war which produced few heroes, Winfield Scott won the applause of the public and was brevetted a major general.

Between the War of 1812 and the next major conflict, the Mexican War, Scott did some writing (on military tactics and temperance), a little fighting (the Blackhawk War and the Seminole War), and much peacemaking (with Canada twice, with South Carolina, and with the Cherokee Nation). In 1841, General Scott was made general in chief of the army and did much to modernize and humanize the military service.

Upon the outbreak of the Mexican War, Scott remained in Washington directing the over-all military effort, while Zachary Taylor was winning victories along the Rio Grande and northern Mexico. However, since Taylor's victories were not bringing the war any closer to an end, Scott devised the plan of attacking Mexico City from the east by landing at Vera Cruz. After Vera Cruz capitulated (March 26, 1847), Scott started his drive for Mexico City that resulted in a brilliant five-months' overland campaign. Consecutive victories at Cerro Gordo (April 18), Contreras (August 19-20), Churubusco (August 20), Molino del Rey (September 8), Chapultepec (September 13), and Mexico City (September 14, 1847) won the war. His conduct as commander of the occupied Mexican capitol so impressed the local government officials that they offered him the dictatorship of the nation.

In 1852, the Whigs nominated Scott for President, but he was badly defeated by the darkhorse Democratic nominee, Franklin Pierce. This was Scott's last real bid for the White House, although he nursed hopes for the presidency through the 1860 election. In 1855, Winfield Scott was appointed a lieutenant general in the regular army, the first officer to hold that high rank since George Washington. In 1859, as in the 1830's, he was called on again to bring peace, this time in the far northwest between the United States, Canada, and Britain. Again he was successful.

Seeing the clouds of sectional strife approaching, General Scott pleaded in vain with President Buchanan and Secretary of War Floyd to re-enforce the Federal forts and armories located in the South. After the outbreak of war, Scott devised the famous "Anaconda Plan"—a strategic plan to strangle the Southern states by blockading the Southern ports and by gaining control of the Mississippi River. On October 31, 1861, the general, now seventy-five and infirm, requested retirement. President Lincoln himself went to Scott's home on the day of retirement and read a moving tribute to the old soldier, a soldier who had been associated with every President from Jefferson to Lincoln.

Lieutenant General Winfield Scott died at West Point on May 29, 1866, within a few days of his eightieth birthday. Known primarily as a great general, Scott was also a great peacemaker and a friend of mankind. Few American soldiers have reached his stature.

(*Dictionary of American Biography, op. cit.,* VIII, 505-11. Warner, *Blue, op. cit.,* 429-30.)

[10]While Taylor was concentrating his forces in the vicinity of Saltillo and Monterrey, the commander in chief of the army, General Winfield Scott, was organizing an army to take Mexico City via an amphibious landing at Vera Cruz. Lee, who wanted to see combat action, was happy to receive orders the middle of January, 1847, to join Scott's Army at Brazos de Santiago (near the mouth of the Rio Grande), where the senior army general was gathering ships and supplies.

Lee, astride his favorite Mexican War mount, Creole (who was not destined to gain the fame that Traveller did in the Civil War), rode the 250 miles across northern Mexico to Scott's headquarters, reporting in late January. Lee's orders to join Scott appear to have been unsolicited. Neither is there written evidence that Scott had asked for Lee by name, although he knew Lee (see note number five). It is possible that Colonel Totten, the senior engineering officer on Scott's staff for whom Lee had worked in the winter of 1844-45, had suggested the Virginian's name to the commander.

If Captain Lee had remained with Taylor's army he would have seen action within a few weeks. Santa Anna, with 15,000 men, attacked Taylor's force of fewer than 5,000 men at Buena Vista on February 22-23, 1847. Buena Vista was an American victory with two of Lee's fellow West Pointers, Jefferson Davis and Braxton Bragg, playing key roles in the smashing success. However, as an engineering officer on Scott's staff, Lee was to see much more action later as the "Vera Cruz Army" drove toward the Mexican capitol.

The transfer to General Scott's Army was one of the major turning points in the career of Robert E. Lee. It brought him to the attention of a man who was to be the commander in chief of the army for more than twenty years. Too, Lee learned much from Scott during the Mexico City campaign, much that he would apply with equal success in the campaigns of the Army of Northern Virginia in the Civil War. (Freeman, *op. cit.*, I, 217-19.)

[11]The battle of Contreras was fought on August 19-20, 1847. Thanks to a rupture in relations between the Mexican commander, Santa Anna, and one of his subordinate generals, the politically potent Gabriel Valencia, the American Army won a crucial victory. Contreras was fought just seven miles from the Mexican capitol and paved the way for Scott's advance into the environs of Mexico City and the eventual capture of that city a few weeks later.

Valencia, contrary to orders, occupied a strong, advanced position—an isolated hill between the villages of Contreras and Padierna not far from the American lines. A massive lava bed, fifteen miles square, known as the Pedregal (a wild tangle of ravines and gullies well nigh impassable for cavalry and artillery) protected Valencia's left flank. Scott determined to cut Valencia's force from the main Mexican Army under Santa Anna by enveloping his left flank, thus closing Valencia's road of retreat toward Mexico City.

Due to the ingenuity and persistence of Engineer Lee (accompanied by Lieutenant P. T. G. Beauregard) a way was found through the Pedregal wilderness, which enabled Scott to carry out his flanking movement and isolate Valencia's exposed force. Scott sent the brigades of Lieutenant Colonel Bennett Riley, Brigadier General George Cadwalader, and Brigadier General Persifor S. Smith through the Pedregal to outflank and attack Valencia's position from the rear at dawn on August 20. Meanwhile Brigadier General Franklin Pierce's Brigade was to pin the Mexican force down by a frontal attack. Lee, during this maneuvering, performed valuable liaison work by crossing the Pedregal several times during the night of the nineteenth to coordinate the early-morning attack. The enveloping movement was successful, the fighting lasted less than twenty minutes; the Mexicans broke and fled down the road toward Churubusco and Mexico City.

Santa Anna, advancing from the vicinity of Churubusco, was not in time to save Valencia from destruction. The Mexican dictator's relief army was all but swept aside by the disorganized rabble of wild-eyed soldiers, confused camp followers, fleeing laborers, stampeding mules, and galloping lancers driven before the victorious Americans. Battle booty included 800 Mexican prisoners (including four generals), numerous horses, 700 mules, large quantities of ammunition, and twenty-two artillery pieces. The Mexican dead alone numbered 700, against an American loss of seventy killed and wounded. The victory drove Santa Anna into the inner defenses around Mexico City.

Lee was praised profusely by General Scott for his work at Contreras, receiving a brevet to lieutenant colonel for gallantry.

(Bill, *op. cit.*, 272-77. Henry, *op. cit.*, 330-37. *The West Point Atlas of American Wars*, Colonel Vincent J. Esposito (chief ed.), (2 vols.; New York: Frederick A. Praeger, 1959), I, Map 16.)

[12]James Shields, one of the most remarkable Irish-Americans of the nineteenth century, was born in County Tyrone, Ireland, on May 12, 1806. He received a good classical education and some formal military training in Irish schools.

Shields emigrated to the United States in 1826 and settled at Kaskaskia, Illinois. He studied law, became a Democrat, and fought in the Blackhawk War (1832-33). In 1836 he was elected a member of the state legislature and later was appointed auditor of the State of Illinois. Governor Thomas Ford named Shields to the Illinois Supreme Court in 1843, and two years later he was appointed commissioner of the General Land Office in Washington by President James K. Polk.

On the outbreak of the Mexican War, Shields resigned his Washington commissionership and was appointed a brigadier general of volunteers on July 1, 1846. During the war he commanded the 1st Brigade in John A. Quitman's Division. Shields' Mexican War record was commendable. At Cerra Gordo (April 18, 1847) he was badly wounded, brevetted a major general, and cited for bravery by General Scott. He led a charge of his brigade of New York Irishmen and South Carolinians at Churubusco (August 20, 1847) that helped to pave the way for an American victory. Early in 1848 Shields' Brigade was deactivated, and he returned to his law practice in Illinois.

James Shields was appointed governor of the Oregon Territory by President Polk in 1848, but resigned almost immediately to accept an election to the United States Senate from Illinois. He served in this capacity until 1855, when he was defeated for re-election by Lyman Trumbull. Following his political defeat in Illinois, Shields moved to Minnesota, where he was instrumental in starting an Irish movement into the area. Upon the admission of Minnesota (in 1858) as the thirty-second state Shields was elected to the short term (expired March 3, 1859) in the United States Senate. The Republican State Legislature failed to re-elect the popular Democrat. After his political defeat in Minnesota, the congenial Irish-American went to California, where he resided briefly and then emigrated to Mexico.

After the surrender of Fort Sumter, Shields offered his services to Lincoln (whom he had once challenged to a duel). The President appointed him a brigadier general of volunteers on August 19, 1861. Shields campaigned in the Shenandoah Valley and fought in the battles of Winchester (May 25, 1862) and Port Republic, or Cross Keys (June 8-9, 1862). He resigned his commission on March 28, 1863, and went to California, where he was appointed state railroad commissioner. He moved to Missouri in 1866 and was elected to fill out an unexpired term in the United States Senate from January 27 to March 3, 1879.

James Shields died June 1, 1879, and was buried at Carrollton, Missouri. He was the only man to represent three different states in the United States Senate.

(Freeman, *op. cit.*, I, 251. *Dictionary of American Biography*, *op. cit.*, IX, 106-07. Boatner, *op. cit.*, 752, 936, 210. Warner, *Blue*, *op. cit.*, 444-45.)

[13]Persifor Frazier Smith was born in Philadelphia on November 16, 1798. He was graduated from the College of New Jersey (now Princeton) and soon afterward went to New Orleans, where he opened a law office. Smith soon became involved in military affairs in the Pelican State, commanding first a company and then a battalion in the Louisiana state militia. His military ability was soon recognized and he was appointed adjutant general of the state troops. As a colonel, Smith led a Louisiana regiment of volunteers in the Seminole War (1836-42).

At the outbreak of the Mexican War, Persifor F. Smith was commissioned a colonel in the United States Army. He fought with Taylor's Army at Monterrey (September 21-24, 1846) and was brevetted to brigadier general for bravery. Smith was transferred to General Scott's Army in the winter of 1846-47, and given command of the new regiment of mounted rifles. Later, during the campaign for Mexico City, he commanded the 1st Brigade (1st Artillery, dismounted; 3rd U. S. Infantry Rifle Regiment; and Taylor's Battery) in David E. Twigg's Division. General Smith distinguished himself at the battles of Contreras (August 19-20, 1847), Churubusco (August 20, 1847), Chapultepec (September 13, 1847), and the capture of Belen Gate (September 14, 1847) at Mexico City. For his "gallant and meritorious conduct" at these engagements, Smith was brevetted to major general. Following the capture of Mexico City, General Smith served for a while as the military governor of the Mexican capitol. He commanded Vera Cruz during the embarkation of U. S. troops from Mexico during the summer of 1848.

Following the war Persifor Smith served as the commander of various military departments — Pacific (1848-50), Texas (1850-56), West (1856-58). He was promoted to a regular brigadier general on December 30, 1856. Smith died on May 17,

1858, while organizing his forces at Fort Leavenworth to take over the Department of Utah.

General Persifor F. Smith was an outstanding soldier and gentleman. He had a magnetic personality, and his commanding presence was an inspiration to his troops. As Smith rode on the field at Contreras, he was greeted enthusiastically with the cries "Here he is!" and "Now we'll have them!" He then proceeded to lead the attack that forced the Mexicans from the field.

(Bill, *op. cit.*, 263, 308, 324. Henry, *op. cit.*, 73, 345. Freeman, *op. cit.*, I, 251, 293, 386. *Dictionary of American Biography, op. cit.*, IX, 331-32.)

[14]George Cadwalader was born in Philadelphia on May 16, 1806, to a financially and socially prominent family. He was a lawyer by training and profession, but he also interested himself in local militia matters.

At the outset of the Mexican War, Cadwalader was appointed a brigadier general of volunteers. He commanded the 1st Brigade (Voltigeur Regiment, 11th and 14th U. S. Infantry Regiments, and a light battery) in Gideon Pillow's Division during Scott's drive on Mexico City. Cadwalader was breveted to major general for his gallantry at Chapultepec (September 13, 1847).

On April 16, 1861, he was appointed a major general of Pennsylvania state troops and on April 25, 1862, was commissioned a major general of United States volunteers. Cadwalader saw very little field action during the Civil War, serving mostly in garrison commands, on boards of inquiry, on various special commissions, and as a special advisor to the President and to the Secretary of War. He resigned on July 5, 1865.

General Cadwalader died on February 3, 1879, and was buried in Philadelphia.

(Henry, *op. cit.*, 255. Bill, *op. cit.*, 257. Freeman, *op. cit.*, I, 251. Mark M. Boatner, *The Civil War Dictionary*, (New York: David McKay Co., Inc., 1959), 112. Warner, *Blue, op. cit.*, 63.)

[15]Robert E. Lee received three brevet promotions for outstanding service during the Mexican War. His first brevet promotion was to major to date from April 18, 1847, "for gallant and meritorious conduct in the Battle of Cerro Gordo." On August 20, 1847, Lee received a brevet promotion to lieutenant

colonel "for felicitous execution as for science and daring" (said General Scott) in the battles of Contreras and Churubusco. His third and last brevet promotion was to the rank of colonel and was dated September 13, 1847, for his conduct at the Battle of Chapultepec.

(Freeman, *op. cit.*, I, 248, 272, 285, 303.)

[16]Fort Carroll was built on a shoal located in midstream between Sollers' Point Flats and Hawkins' Point, halfway between Baltimore and the mouth of the Patapsco River. Its purpose was to defend the city of Baltimore.

The site for the proposed fort was selected in 1847, and preliminary work was started in the spring of 1848. Captain Lee was assigned to the project on September 13, 1848, and reported for duty at Baltimore on November 18.

Until October 8, 1850, the partially finished fort was referred to merely as "the fort at Sollers' Point Flats." After this date it was officially named Fort Carroll in honor of Charles Carroll, a Marylander and the last surviving signer of the Declaration of Independence. Carroll died at the age of ninety-five in 1832.

Lee remained with the Fort Carroll project until late May, 1852, when he received orders transferring him to West Point as superintendent. The fort was well along toward completion when Lee was transferred from Baltimore.

(Freeman, *op. cit.*, I, 303-09, 316.)

[17]The Cubans revolted several times during the nineteenth century against their Spanish overlords. All of the revolts were put down ruthlessly. During these revolutions Cuban insurgent groups collectively called "junta" operated openly from the United States, where public opinion generally was sympathetic to the Cuban cause.

The revolt to which Davis refers broke out in 1848 and was headed by a former colonel in the Spanish Army, Narcisco Lopez. Lopez insisted that a high-ranking American officer lead the insurgent invasion force that was to wrest "the Pearl of the Antilles" from the Spaniards. To the "Club of Havana" and the "Cuban Counselors," two member organizations of the Cuban junta in New York, was given the task of selecting the American leader. A total price of three million dollars in gold (so much down, so much monthly) was the amount promised to the American officer who would successfully lead the Cubans to freedom.

General William "Haughty Bill" Worth was the first American the Cubans approached. He was considering the proposition but died before he could make up his mind. The insurgents then contacted Jefferson Davis, a senator from Mississippi at the time, Chairman of the Committee on Military Affairs, and an avowed supporter of Cuban freedom. Davis declined the junta's offer but referred the selection committee to Robert E. Lee. The group concurred in Davis' choice and journeyed to Baltimore to offer Engineer Lee the precarious command; hence the Virginian's trip to Washington to consult with Senator Davis. Upon Lee's declination, the command of the expedition was offered to General John A. Quitman, who at the time (1849) was the governor-elect of Mississippi. Quitman was extremely interested in the "deal" but finally refused the command.

Lopez and his fellow Cubans were not successful in engaging an outstanding American soldier to command the expedition back to the island. Late in 1849, after Quitman refused, a Colonel White was selected, but after organizing an invasion force of some 800 insurgents at New Orleans, White backed out and left the revolutionary force stranded at the Crescent City. Lopez led three abortive attempts during the next two years to land and arouse the Cuban patriots. Finally, in the summer of 1851, William Crittenden, a nephew of John J. Crittenden, Attorney General for Millard Fillmore, was induced to share command privileges with Lopez. The fourth and last expedition during this particular revolt (1848-51) was a fiasco. Narcisco Lopez was captured and hanged, and Crittenden fled back to safety in the United States without making much of an attempt to support Lopez's wing of the invasion force.

The most prolonged struggle of the Cuban insurgents during the century was the so-called Ten Years War, which began in 1868 under the leadership of Carlos Manuel de Céspedes. President Grant took an unusual interest in the Céspedes-led revolt and pressed for recognition of the insurgents until persuaded otherwise by his Secretary of State, Hamilton Fish.

The last of the Cuban uprisings led by Masó, Gómez, García, and Martí in 1895, eventually led to the Spanish-American War and ultimate freedom for the persistent Cubans.

(Carlos Marquez Sterling, *Historia de Cuba,* (New York: Las Americas Publishing Co., 1963), 111-118. *Dictionary of American History,* James Truslow Adams (ed.), (6 vols., 2nd edit.; New York: Charles Scribner's Sons, 1940), II, 93-94. Freeman, *op. cit.,* I, 306-07. *Dictionary of American Biography, op. cit.,* VIII, 315-16.)

[18]Both Presidents Taylor and Fillmore assured the Spanish Government that it was the wish and intent of the United States to recognize all Spanish treaties and Spanish authority over Cuba.

It is interesting to note that Jefferson Davis, by using the verb tense "were" instead of "was," referred to the United States as being several entities instead of one unified body. He was an "unreconstructed rebel" and states righter to the very end.

(Sterling, *op. cit.,* 111-115.)

[19]Jefferson Davis served as Secretary of War from 1853 to 1857 in the cabinet of Franklin Pierce. He was particularly interested in the United States Military Academy (his alma mater) and made numerous improvements in the curriculum. It was Davis' thought that West Point should be more than a technical school; hence at his suggestion subjects like English literature, history, ethics, and logic were added to the course of study. Secretary Davis, in order to encourage "cultural" courses of this nature, effected an extension of the whole Military Academy course from four years to five years. Even after he left the secretaryship, and as a senator, Davis continued his interest in a broader education for the West Point cadet. In a letter to President Buchanan, Jefferson Davis declared: "It has long been the subject of remark that the graduates of the Military Academy whilst occupying the first rank as scholars in the exact sciences were below mediocrity in polite literature. Their official reports frequently exhibited poverty of style."

Secretary of War Davis promoted many other military efficiencies and innovations while in office. Among other things, the Mississippian introduced an improved system of infantry tactics, the rifled musket, the minie ball, improved the recruiting service, increased the pay of privates and bettered their living conditions, put the manufacturing of arms under the War Department, set in motion several meteorological and geological surveys, expanded the army, strengthened the frontier defenses, introduced the camel into the army, promoted soldier education at military posts, and improved the artillery carriage.

Although Jefferson Davis filled many offices of high public trust, his greatest public service was performed as Secretary of War. He must rank with Calhoun and Root as the outstanding Secretaries of War in United States history.

(John Crane and James F. Keiley, *West Point, Key to America,* (New York: McGraw Hill Book Company, Inc., 1947), 84-5. Hudson Strode, *Jefferson Davis, American Patriot,* (New York: Harcourt, Brace and Co., 1955), 260-80.)

[20]Brevet Colonel Robert E. Lee succeeded Captain Henry Brewerton as superintendent of the United States Military Academy on September 1, 1852, and thus became the ninth superintendent in the history of West Point. Lee left the superintendency on March 31, 1855, and was succeeded by Brevet Major Jonathan G. Barnard.

Several officers who would gain fame in the Civil War were serving in key staff positions at the Academy while Lee was superintendent. Major George "Rock of Chickamauga" Thomas was the senior instructor in infantry and cavalry, Major Robert S. Garnett (who would be the first general officer killed in the war) was the commandant of cadets, and Brevet Captain Seth Williams and Captain Fitz John Porter served as adjutants of the Academy, the latter succeeding the former about half way through Lee's tenure.

Too, many cadets who were graduated during the Virginian's superintendency became outstanding leaders in the fratricidal struggle of the following decade. John B. McPherson, Phillip Sheridan, and John Bell Hood were among the graduates of the Class of 1853, Lee's first class as superintendent. With the Class of 1854, Lee saw his own son, G. W. Custis Lee, graduated number one followed by such future military greats as Oliver Otis Howard, John Pegram, James Ewell Brown (JEB) Stuart, Stephan Dill Lee (no relation to Robert E.), and Dorsey Pender.

Three cadets in particular gave Lee many of the gray hairs that Jefferson Davis noted. His own nephew, Fitz Lee, was close to being dismissed from the Academy twice for tomfoolery; James McNeill Whistler, who would later gain fame as a painter, was dismissed finally for excessive demerits, and Archibald Gracie III, who had a propensity for fighting, gave the superintendent a few anxious moments.

(Freeman *op. cit.,* I, 319-40.)

[21]After lengthy debates in both the House and the Senate, the establishment of two new cavalry regiments (1st and 2nd) and two new infantry regiments (9th and 10th) was finally authorized. The President signed the activation bill on March 3, 1855. Leading the attack against the increase to the army had been Senators Sam Houston (Texas) and Thomas Hart Benton (Missouri). Ironically one of the new regiments, the 2nd Cavalry, would be posted to Houston's home state to guard the frontier there against the Comanches. Senator James Shields (Illinois) led the successful fight for the augmentation to the regular forces (see note number 12).

(George F. Price, *Across the Continent With the Fifth Cavalry*, (New York: Antaquarian Press, Ltd., 1959), 11-20. Spaulding, *op. cit.*, 232.)

[22]The 2nd U. S. Cavalry Regiment was one of the four new regiments authorized on March 3, 1855. It was established particularly for service on the Texas frontier; and because Jefferson Davis, Secretary of War in Pierce's cabinet, fostered the regiment, it was sometimes known as "Jeff Davis' Own." The officers were selected personally by the Secretary of War from the regular army regiments as well as from the Texas Rangers and other famous law enforcement bodies. The 2nd Cavalry was an elite organization from its commander and deputy commander, Colonel Albert Sidney Johnston and Brevet Colonel Robert E. Lee, down to its lowest ranking 2nd lieutenant, Robert C. Wood, Jr. The senior officers recommended and selected the noncommissioned officers, and they, too, were the best in the mounted service. The horses for the regiment were purchased by a special team of 2nd Cavalry officers who had been instructed to select only the best blooded stock in Kentucky, Indiana, and Ohio. Each company was to ride horses of one color. Grays were procured for Company A; sorrels for Companies B and E; bays for Companies C, D, F, and I; browns for Companies G and H; and roans for Company K. On dress parade the regiment was magnificent. It later proved itself as superb in fighting on the frontier as it was in prancing on the parade ground.

Probably no other regiment in United States history spawned so many general officers as did the 2nd Cavalry. It was studded with stars. Of approximately forty officers assigned to the regiment during its short life, four became full generals in the Confederacy: Albert Sidney Johnston, Robert E. Lee, Edmund Kirby Smith, and John Bell Hood. Hence, this one regiment contributed half of the four-star generals in the Confederate service. One officer, William J. Hardee, rose to three-star rank under the Stars and Bars; three—Earl Van Dorn, Charles W. Field, and Fitzhugh Lee—attained two-star status; and three—Nathan "Shanks" Evans, James P. Major, and George B. Cosby—won brigadier stars in the Southern army. Of those officers of the 2nd Cavalry who remained in the Federal service, four became generals, all winning two stars— George H. Thomas, Kenner Garrard, George Stoneman, Jr., and Richard W. Johnson. The remaining officers of the regiment who fought in the war were promoted to high field grade rank, the majority of them to the rank of full colonel.

(Price, *op. cit.*, 26-31.)

[23]Although Lee had enjoyed his work with the Corps of Engineers and although it was an honor to be associated with what many people regarded as the elite branch of the military service, the future, as far as possibility of promotion, was bleak. Although sixty-seven, General Totten, the chief of the corps, was in good health and not contemplating retirement. Ahead of the Virginian on the promotion list of the corps of engineers were two lieutenant colonels, four majors, and three captains. On the other hand, the majority of the general officers and colonels in the artillery, cavalry, and infantry were old and ready for retirement and there was talk of increasing the authorization for generals in those branches of the service. Hence, promotion opportunities appeared much brighter outside of the engineers. Lee, however, had no choice but to follow the order transferring him to the cavalry—the Secretary of War had hand-picked him for the assignment.

(Freeman, *op. cit.*, I, 349-50.)

[24]In the summer of 1857, President Buchanan ordered a large military expedition into Utah to accompany the newly-appointed Federal civilian officials for that area. The Mormons, who had settled Utah, refused to recognize the authority of the United States, refused to circulate United States money in their area, and had incited the Indians against other white settlers on the frontier. This direct challenge to the sovereignty of the

United States did not go unheeded. Brevet Brigadier General Albert Sidney Johnston was in command of the military force sent to chastise the followers of Brigham Young. Johnston's force consisted of eight companies of the 2nd Dragoons, the 5th and 10th Infantry Regiments, a six-pounder battery of the 4th Artillery, and a twelve-pounder battery manned by members of the Ordnance Department.

The punitive expedition reached the border of Utah in October, 1857, and was opposed by a large force of militant Mormons—more interested now in pillaging than in praying. Young's followers "committed actual acts of war by driving off animals, burning supply trains, and seizing and imprisoning members of the force." The army remained the winter of 1857-58 at Fort Bridger pending negotiations between Brigham Young and Federal civilian representatives. The winter was cold and difficult and necessitated the dispatch of a column south to New Mexico under Captain Randolph B. Marcy to procure food and supplies.

In the spring of 1858 a large relief column of some three thousand men concentrated at Fort Leavenworth and marched to the aid of Johnston. In June, with a combined army of 5,500, Albert Sidney Johnston moved into the Salt Lake Valley. The Mormons, overwhelmed by the force of infantry, cavalry and artillery sent against them, quickly reached an agreement with the new Federal governor of the Utah Territory. Johnston's "Army of Utah" was gradually dispersed and assigned to other duties. Johnston, himself, stayed on as military commander of the Department of Utah.

(Spaulding, *op. cit.*, 236-39. John K. Herr and Edward S. Wallace, *The Story of the U.S. Cavalry, 1775-1942,* (Boston: Little Brown & Co., 1953), 83-84. Ezra Warner, *Generals in Gray,* (Baton Rouge: Louisiana State University Press, 1959), 159-60.)

[25]Lee assumed command of the 2nd Cavalry at San Antonio, Texas, on July 29, 1857, and replaced Colonel Albert Sidney Johnston who was ordered to Washington for assignment as commander of the Utah Expedition. Lee remained in command of the famed cavalry regiment at this time for only a few months. On October 24, 1857, he left San Antonio on two months' emergency leave orders for Virginia. Lee's father-in-law, G. W. P. Custis, had died suddenly on October 10, leaving

Mrs. Lee (his daughter), now a semi-invalid, alone at the Arlington mansion. Lee, of course, wanted to see to his wife's welfare. Too, as executor of the estate, Lee's presence was required in Virginia.

The senior major of the 2nd Cavalry, George H. Thomas, succeeded to temporary command of the regiment in Lee's absence. The regimental headquarters was moved at this time from San Antonio to Fort Mason, Texas (Mason County), where Thomas was post commander. Inasmuch as Lee asked for and was granted several extensions to his original leave orders, Major Thomas remained in "temporary" command of the regiment for over three years.

(Freeman, *op. cit.*, I, 377-78. Special Order No. 136, Hq. Department of Texas, dated October 21, 1857, Records of the Department of Texas, National Archives, Washington, D. C. Post Returns for Fort Mason, Texas, 1857-1861, Records of the Department of Texas, National Archives, Washington, D. C.)

[26]Lee, who was on a leave of absence from his regiment trying to clear up his father-in-laws' estate, was notified at Arlington, Virginia, on the morning of October 17, 1859, to report to the War Department immediately. Lieutenant JEB Stuart, who happened to be in Washington at the time on personal business, carried the message out to Arlington. The urgent dispatch was in relation to John Brown's raid on Harper's Ferry, Virginia. Lee, not having had time to change into his uniform, reported to the Secretary of War in civilian clothes. He was ordered by President Buchanan to take command of all available Federal and state military forces and put down the "insurrection."

Accompanied by eager, young Lieutenant Stuart, Lee was taken by special train to Harper's Ferry. Taking command of a detachment of U. S. Marines under Lieutenant Israel Green and four companies of Maryland militia, Colonel Lee, on the evening of October 17, crossed the Potomac River to the site of the government arsenal near where the local population had brought "Pottawatomie" Brown to bay. Brown and his followers (holding several hostages) had barricaded themselves inside of the fire engine house.

Believing that this was an insurrection against a state and not the United States, Lee gave the Maryland and the Virginia militia companies (the latter had arrived shortly after Lee) the privilege of volunteering for the assault against the fire engine house. Both commanders immediately declined, pleading that they were not being paid for that type of employment and that they had small children and wives at home. Lieutenant Green and his U. S. Marines, on the other hand, jumped at the opportunity to lead the assault. Before attacking Brown, Lee sent Stuart under a flag of truce to the white-bearded fanatic with a letter asking him to surrender peacefully, and he would be protected by the Federal government. If Brown refused to capitulate, Stuart had been instructed to raise his hat; and Lee would order Lieutenant Green to attack. Brown, after reading Colonel Lee's short letter, commenced to argue with Stuart over the evils of slavery. The red-haired Virginia lieutenant, refusing to be drawn into a long debate on slavery, waved his hat. In three minutes the affair was over. Brown and all of his followers were either captured or killed, and the thirteen hostages were released unharmed. Colonel Lee turned the insurrectionists over to the Virginia State officials and returned to Washington with his command (marines and Maryland militia) early on the morning of October 20, 1859.

The commander of the 2nd Cavalry was not able to leave Virginia to rejoin his regiment in Texas until early February, 1860. Lee had to remain in the East several months after the John Brown Raid to participate in the investigation that followed the affair.

(Freeman, *op. cit.,* I, 394-404. Laurence Green, *The Raid,* (New York: Henry Holt and Company, 1953), 145, 164-73, 185.)

[27]Robert E. Lee was assigned back to the Lone Star State (after his much-extended leave had expired) on February 6, 1860, as the temporary commander of the Department of Texas with headquarters at San Antonio. He realized that this assignment would be of short duration—only until the next brigadier general was assigned to the department.

Lee journeyed to Texas via New Orleans, landing at Indianola at noon on February 19 and was at San Antonio two days later. On February 22, he assumed command of the Department of Texas. Lee, no doubt preoccupied with the disability of his wife, the litigation concerning the Arlington estate, and the growing tension over slavery, discovered at New Orleans that he had left two very essential items at home—his shaving brush and his extra pair of trousers.

While Colonel Lee was in temporary command of the Department of Texas several major problems arose that made his
desk assignment anything but relaxing. Juan Cortinas, the
self-styled "Robin Hood of the Rio Grande," raided along the
lower Rio Grande Valley, melting into the Mexican mesquite and
mountains when pursued. The Kiowas and Comanches raided
close to Camps Colorado (Coleman County) and Cooper
(Throckmorton County) on the frontier, driving off livestock
and attacking isolated ranchers. Secession talk was in the air,
and the Knights of the Golden Circle were active in San Antonio, one of the strongholds of the Texas secessionists.

With the return of General David E. Twiggs in mid-Decem-
ber, 1860, Lee relinquished temporary command of the Department and left for Fort Mason, headquarters of the 2nd Cavalry.
He arrived at Fort Mason on December 22 and resumed command of his regiment after a lapse of three years and two
months.

(Freeman, *op. cit.*, I, 404-18. Post Returns for Fort Mason, Texas,
op. cit., 1859-61.)

[28]On February 1, 1861, the Texas Secession Convention
meeting in Austin passed an ordinance of secession by the over-
whelming vote of 166 to 7. During the roll call for voting, one
of the non-secessionists, James "Old Leathercoat" Throckmorton, arose, voted against secession; and then, amid catcalls and
hisses, he proclaimed in a loud voice so that the galleries could
hear, "Mr. President, when the rabble hiss well may patriots
tremble." Once the die was cast, however, Throckmorton supported the Confederacy wholeheartedly, serving in numerous
key civilian and military positions. The vote of the convention
was sustained by the electorate later in the month by more than
a three-to-one majority. Texas was out of the Union and in the
Confederacy by March 4, 1861.

Colonel Lee, in January 1861, confided to one of his company commanders (Captain Richard W. Johnson) that he would
defend Fort Mason against an attempt by a Texas secessionist
force to seize it. He even disclosed to Captain Johnson the plan
of defense that he had formulated. Whether Lee's plan of defense pertained just to Fort Mason or involved the other forts
where units of his command, the 2nd Cavalry, were stationed

is not known. However, before the Texas secessionists committed an overt act toward Fort Mason, Lee had received orders to report to General Scott in Washington, and his contemplated plan was never put into operation. Colonel Lee left Fort Mason on February 13 and left Texas via San Antonio (where he was shocked to see the rebellious efforts of the Texans) and Indianola for Washington, where he was due to report by April 1.

Lee reached his Arlington home on March 1. Soon afterwards, probably the next day, he reported to General Scott. The two were closeted together for some three hours. The commander in chief of the Federal Army offered Lee promotion to full colonel and promised to recommend to the Secretary of War that the Virginian be appointed second in command to him. Lee demurred, saying that if Virginia seceded his first honor was to his native state. Scott suggested that Lee think the matter over, but should he not want to fight for the United States Government he should consider resigning his commission.

With the dismissal of General D. E. Twiggs on March 1, 1861, from the United States Army (for his surrender of the United States forts in Texas), Colonel E. V. Sumner, commander of the 1st U. S. Cavalry Regiment, was promoted to brigadier general; Lee was made a full colonel (to fill Sumner's vacancy) and given command of the 1st Cavalry Regiment. President Lincoln signed Colonel Lee's commission which was forwarded to him at Arlington on March 28 and which he accepted immediately. Lee, in the meanwhile, had been offered a brigadier general's commission in the Confederate Army by Davis' Secretary of War, Leroy P. Walker. He ignored this Confederate offer; Lee was still a Virginian first and a United States officer second; he was not interested in a third political unity unless Virginia should become a part of it.

On April 17 Lee received a letter from General Scott requesting that he come over to see the army commander the following day. Enclosed with Scott's note was a note from Lee's cousin in Washington, John Lee, who wanted the Colonel to see Francis P. Blair, Sr., before he saw Scott. Behind the scenes President Lincoln, Montgomery Blair, Sr., and Secretary of War Cameron had been working to keep Lee in a blue uniform. It was agreed that Colonel Robert E. Lee should be offered the command of the large Union army that was soon to be put into the field to enforce Federal law. It was to tell him this that

Blair had requested to see Lee before he saw Scott. Although sorely tempted to accept the Federal offer, an offer which would have fulfilled all of his career ambitions, he declined to command an army he said that was to invade his native state and the other Southern states. Calling upon Scott shortly after seeing Blair, Lee told his old commander of the offer and of his refusal to accept it. Scott, disappointed, remarked that Lee had made "the greatest mistake of his life" and again advised him that if he proposed to resign it would be proper to do so at once.

The Old Dominion State was one of the last states to enter the Confederacy, and she did so only after much hesitation. On January 12, 1861, a special session of the General Assembly of Virginia voted for the election of a convention to decide the secession issue. On February 4 the people elected delegates to this convention; the delegates that were chosen were two to one against secession. The Virginia electorate also voted at this time (February 4) that no ordinance of secession would be valid unless sustained by the voters of the state in a general election.

The special secession convention convened at Richmond on February 13, and, as expected, voted against secession. As late as April 4, a test vote of members of the Virginia convention showed that a majority of two to one of the delegates were still against secession. On April 16, the Virginia convention went into secret session and passed the Ordinance of Secession the following day. The convention did not, however, publicly announce the decision until after they had given orders to seize the major Federal facilities within the state boundaries. By the nineteenth the Washington papers had announced the fact. The Virginia voters did not ratify the Ordinance of Secession until May 23. On the following day Union troops invaded the Old Dominion State.

Robert E. Lee realized that the pro-secession vote of the people's representatives at the Convention meant that Virginia had left the Union. As a soldier he could not wait for an undetermined number of weeks for the electorate to sustain the verdict; the decision would, no doubt, stand. After much soul-searching and pacing the floor Colonel Lee, on the morning of April 20, sent his resignation from the United States Army to Secretary of War Simon Cameron. After four years of cadet-ship and almost thirty-two years of active duty, his service under the stars and stripes was over. At the same time that he wrote to Secretary Cameron, Lee penned a short letter to his old friend, General Winfield Scott, thanking him for his consideration and kindness over the years. Lee left for Richmond on April 22. On April 23 he accepted the command of the military forces of Virginia. Lee had seceded with his state.

(Robert Selph Henry, *The Story of the Confederacy,* (New York: Grosset & Dunlap, 1936), 35-36. Carl Coke Rister, *Robert E. Lee in Texas,* (Norman: University of Oklahoma Press, 1946), 96-167. Richard W. Johnson, *A Soldier's Reminiscences in Peace and War,* (Philadelphia: J. B. Lippincott Co., 1886), 132-33.)

[29]Lee's letters to his sister (Mrs. Marshall) and to General Winfield Scott follow:

Arlington, Virginia, April 20, 1861

My Dear Sister:

I am grieved at my inability to see you. . . . I have been waiting for a "more convenient season," which has brought to many before me deep and lasting regret. Now we are in a state of war which will yield to nothing. The whole South is in a state of revolution, into which Virginia, after a long struggle, has been drawn; and, though I recognize no necessity for this state of things, and would have forborne and pleaded to the end for a redress of grievances, real or supposed, yet in my own person I had to meet the question whether I should take part against my native state.

With all my devotion to the Union and the feeling of loyalty and duty of an American citizen, I have not been able to make up my mind to raise my hand against my relatives, my children, my home. I have therefore resigned my commission in the Army, and save in defence of my native state, with the sincere hope that my poor services may never be needed, I hope I may never be called on to draw my sword. I know you will blame me; but you must think as kindly of me as you can, and believe that I have endeavored to do what I thought right.

To show you the feeling and struggle it has cost me, I send you a copy of my letter of resignation. I have no time for more. May God guard and protect you and yours and shower upon you everlasting blessings, is the prayer of your devoted brother,

R. E. Lee

Arlington, Virginia, April 20, 1861

General:

Since my interview with you on the 18th inst. I have felt that I ought no longer to retain my commission in the Army. I therefore tender my resignation, which I request you will recommend for acceptance. I would have presented it at once, but for the struggle it has cost me to separate myself from a service to which I have devoted all the best years of my life and all the ability I possessed.

During the whole of that time—more than a quarter of a century—I have experienced nothing but kindness from my superiors and a most cordial friendship from my comrades. To no one, General, have I been as much indebted as to yourself for uniform kindness and consideration, and it has always been my ardent desire to meet your approbation. I shall carry to the grave the most grateful recollections of your kind consideration, and your name and fame will always be dear to me.

Save in defence of my native State, I never desire again to draw my sword.

Be pleased to accept my most earnest wishes for the continuance of your happiness and prosperity, and believe me, most truly yours,

R. E. Lee

[30]Around the turn of the twentieth century one of the subjects which was much debated was the decision of Robert E. Lee to resign from the United States Army—to violate his oath of allegiance to defend the United States, and to join in the "rebellion" as a "traitor" against the United States.

The Outlook magazine in 1903 and 1904 carried a series of articles entitled, "The Loyalty of Robert E. Lee," in which writers on both sides aired their views. The editorial staff of *The Outlook* summed up the controversy in a final article in their July 11, 1904 issue. According to the editors of *The Outlook:*

> The test of patriotism, like the test of any other moral quality, is not success, but loyal to conviction; and by that test Robert E. Lee stands today among the purest, though among the most tragically misled and misunderstood of patriots.
> That he chose to follow that high motive which kept

him with his state *The Outlook* believes to have been an error in political judgment; but it was not a moral error, nor even an error of political morality. He who is loyal cannot be a traitor, and Lee and the men of his stamp were as loyal to their conscientious convictions as were the men who fought against them.

To Lee the institutions of his country which he was called upon to defend were those of his native state. To him the Federal constitution was of prime importance politically, but he regarded it as an external compact between his state and the other states, and he believed that the State, not what he regarded as a federation of states, demanded his supreme loyalty.

[31]Robert E. Lee, not counting the four years that he served his country as a cadet at West Point, spent almost thirty-two years on active military service. Thus he had fully repaid the United States Government in active duty time (considering a thirty-year retirement as normal) for the four-year training period that he had received at government expense.

[32]Reference note number 28.

[33]Joseph Eggleston Johnston and Robert E. Lee had been classmates at West Point and were the only two Virginians which were graduated with the Class of 1829. They kept in touch with each other and remained good friends all of their lives.

Joseph E. Johnston was born on February 3, 1807, at Farmville, Virginia. He served with gallantry in both the Seminole (1836-42) and the Mexican (1846-48) Wars. In the latter he was brevetted three times for meritorious service and was wounded twice, once at Cerro Gordo (April 18, 1847) and a second time at Mexico City (September 14, 1847). Johnston was appointed quartermaster general of the U. S. Army in 1860. He resigned from the Federal service several days after Lee and was commissioned a brigadier general in the Confederate Army in May, 1861.

During the Civil War, General Johnston distinguished himself in several campaigns. He came to Beauregard's aid at First Manassas (July 21, 1861); and for his conduct on this field was promoted to full general to rank behind Samuel Cooper, Albert Sidney Johnston, and Robert E. Lee in that order. He commanded the Confederate Army before Richmond during Mc-

Clellan's Peninsular Campaign (April-July, 1862) until severely wounded at Seven Pines (May 31, 1862). Johnston was replaced as commander in Virginia by General Lee. After recovering from his wounds, he was assigned to command the Department of the West in November, 1862. Johnston played a minor role in the Vicksburg Campaign (April-July, 1863). (His objective [which was never realized] was to decoy Grant toward him at Jackson [Mississippi] to relieve the pressure on Pemberton besieged at Vicksburg.) Johnston relieved General Braxton Bragg as commander of the Army of Tennessee after the Chattanooga debacle in November, 1863. He, in turn, was relieved by President Davis—during the Atlanta Campaign (March-August, 1864) for his Fabian tactics against General William T. Sherman. John Bell Hood replaced Johnston July 17, 1864. General J. E. Johnston held no active command after the summer of 1864, until he was assigned late in the war (February, 1865) to oppose Sherman's victorious march through the Carolinas. Johnston surrendered the remnants of the powerful Army of Tennessee to Sherman near Durham Station (North Carolina) on April 28, 1865. Unfortunately for the Confederacy, President Davis and General Johnston feuded during most of the war.

Following the war, Joseph E. Johnston served a term (1879-81) in the U. S. House of Representatives. In 1885 he was appointed the U. S. Commissioner of Railroads by President Grover Cleveland. Johnston held this appointment until his death on March 21, 1891. His death was said to have been brought on by a cold that he had contracted while marching bareheaded in the funeral procession of his old adversary and friend, General William Tecumseh Sherman.

(Warner, *Gray, op. cit.*, 161-62. Boatner, *op. cit.*, 441.)

[34]Davis was mistaken here. The Confederate campaign in the western part of Virginia (the state of West Virginia after 1863) was a complete failure. The terrain, the Unionist sentiment of the local population, the split command responsibilities, and the problem of logistics doomed the Confederate endeavor from the beginning. Even the genius of Robert E. Lee could not save the Southern effort in the foreboding mountains of western Virginia.

The West Virginia campaign was fought during the summer and early fall months of 1861. The Confederate objective in the campaign was to secure the northwestern counties of Virginia. These counties of the Old Dominion State were largely Unionist in sentiment, were composed primarily of small farm holdings in rugged hill and mountain country, and were tied socially and economically to the Ohio River Valley rather than to Tidewater Virginia. The fifty-five counties of northwestern Virginia were organized as a separate state during the Civil War and were admitted to the Federal Union as the State of West Virginia on June 20, 1863.

On May 24, 1861, Union troops under the leadership of the brilliant organizer but timid fighter, General George B. McClellan, crossed the Ohio and advanced down the Baltimore & Ohio Railroad toward Grafton. The purpose of McClellan's advance was to encourage the Union sentiment further in this section of Virginia and to safeguard the Baltimore & Ohio Railroad—an important communications link between the East and the West.

General Robert S. Garnett (who was commandant of cadets at West Point while Lee was the superintendent) commanded the 5,000 Confederate troops in western Virginia. Second in command of the Confederate force was Lieutenant Colonel John Pegram. McClellan, in a series of small engagements at Philippi (June 3), Rich Mountain (July 11), and Carrick's Ford (July 13, 1861), scattered the Confederate force, killing Garnett and capturing Pegram. (Garnett was the first general officer killed on either side during the war.) The remnants of Garnett's and Pegram's force fell back to central Virginia, where they were reinforced by twelve new Confederate regiments, the entire force being placed under the command of General W. W. "Blizzards" Loring. Henry Wise and John Floyd, both former governors of Virginia and now brigadier generals in the Confederate Army, held small independent commands in the West Virginia theater of operations.

Robert E. Lee, former commander of all Virginia armed forces and now a full general in the Confederate Army, was called upon to recoup the prestige of the Confederacy in the western part of Virginia. Lee left Richmond on July 28; his orders were strange; he was to coordinate the Confederate movements, not command operations; but the public was unaware of this. Trying to retain the trans-Alleghany counties of Virginia for the Confederacy was a losing battle. Not only was the populace hostile, but several of the Confederate generals who were commanding splinter forces in the theater were grossly incompetent. Bickering among the senior officers, particularly Floyd and Wise, was the order of the day. Lee didn't have a chance to make a success of his assignment in western Virginia. Besides the major disabilities noted above, the Confederate force was seventy miles from its railhead with only rugged mountain tracks leading back to its base; the rainy season continued throughout the summer; and measles and mumps swept through the wet, chilly camps that lacked even basic hospital facilities.

General William S. Rosecrans, who had replaced the victorious McClellan (now elevated to the command of the Federal Army after his July successes in western Virginia) as the commander of the Union forces, was Lee's opponent during the latter phase of the West Virginia Campaign. Splitting his 20,000-man force into three units, Rosecrans systematically drove the badly outnumbered, demoralized, and confused Confederates from the western counties of Virginia. The Federals defeated Wise at Carnifix Ferry (September 10), and Lee failed to destroy the Federal brigade of Joseph J. Reynolds at Cheat Mountain (September 10-15). By early October, the Kanawha Valley was lost to the Confederates; and soon after, the advent of winter ended the campaigning for 1861.

Lee returned to Richmond on October 31, his prestige at a low ebb, his reputation as the invincible soldier tarnished, and the press howling for his scalp. Lee could have justified his movements and his conduct, but he let the matter drop. Within a year he would vindicate himself by deeds, not words.

(Freeman, *op. cit.*, I, 541-610. Boatner, *op. cit.*, 907-08. Henry, *op. cit.*, 45-48, 64-65.)

[35]An abatis is an obstruction formed by felled trees with the branches (sharpened) pointed outward or toward the enemy. The abatis was quite a common (and effective) defense device used during the Civil War by both sides.

[36]Lee was ridiculed by the Richmond newspapers for his loss of the western counties of Virginia and for the failure of the campaign generally. He was nicknamed "Granny Lee" and "Evacuating Lee" for what appeared to the newspapermen to

have been unnecessarily slow, hesitating movements in western Virginia and for his finally giving up the western counties altogether.

(Freeman, *op. cit.*, I, 602. Henry, *op. cit.*, 65.)

[37]On November 6, 1861, President Davis directed that the coasts of South Carolina, Georgia, and east Florida be constituted a military district or department and appointed General Lee as the department commander. Lee left Richmond for Charleston, South Carolina, on November 6 and arrived the next day. He immediately went to Port Royal Sound. Here a sizeable Union expedition (about 13,000 troops and twenty-five ships) under the joint command of Flag-Officer Samuel F. Du Pont and Brigadier General Thomas W. Sherman was anchored. The Union fleet had arrived off Port Royal Sound on November 4 and had bombarded Confederate forts, Walker and Beauregard, both of which surrendered the day that Lee arrived.

The two most important coastal cities under Lee's jurisdiction were Charleston and Savannah, the former near the northern end of his command and the latter near the southern end. As an emergency plan, to forestall a successful invasion by the Federal force, Lee decided on three defensive courses of action: (1) to prepare the defenses of Charleston and Savannah to sustain a serious bombardment, (2) to obstruct the several rivers up which the Federal fleet might move into the interior, and (3) to assemble the scattered Confederate forces and post them at the most probable points of a Federal landing and subsequent advance inland. Lee's program for defense received support from Governor F. W. Pickens of South Carolina, Governor Joseph E. Brown of Georgia, and Jefferson Davis and prevented the Federals from exploiting their advantage of concentration and position. To accomplish his three objectives, General Lee withdrew all the guns and garrisons from unimportant, outlying positions and established a deep interior defense line that protected the Charleston and Savannah Railroad, the main north-south transportation artery through his command. At the same time he strengthened the defenses around the two major cities within his command, and sunk obsolete vessels in the river channels.

The digging of the interior defense line required close supervision. Once on a single day's inspection trip Lee covered 115 miles, most of it by train, but for thirty-five miles of the journey he rode a beautiful gray horse named "Greenbrier." Because Greenbrier showed so much endurance and strength on these inspection trips, Lee thought him a "fine traveller" and thus he was renamed Traveller and soon became part of the Lee trademark. In the beginning the General established his headquarters at Charleston, as he had started working on the northern end of the inner defense line first. On February 3, 1862, he moved to Savannah, as the work had progressed by that time more than half way to the Georgia seaport.

The loss of Forts Henry and Donelson in Tennessee to Grant in February, 1862, caused the Confederate high command to change its strategy somewhat. Reinforcements from less important theaters were funneled westward in order to bolster the important Confederate defense line in Tennessee. Lee lost some 4,000 men of his sparse command to the Tennessee operation and was ordered to abandon Florida up to the Apalachicola River. Work on the defense line now moved slowly; but happily for the Confederates, the Federals had a timid commander (General Thomas W. Sherman) who was satisfied with occupying Tybee Island at the mouth of the Savannah River.

Fortunately for his career and for the South, Lee was called back to Richmond by President Davis on March 2, and was back in the Confederate capitol on the fourth. Major General John C. Pemberton (later the defender of Vicksburg) succeeded the Virginian in command of the Southeastern Coast Department. Lee had, by the judicial concentration of the scattered force allotted him, by obstructing the major rivers (Santee, Pee Dee, and Savannah), and by the near completion of a stout inner defense line, balked the movement of a combined Federal operation to exploit the South Carolina, Georgia, and northern Florida coastline and immediate hinterland.

Lee had learned several things while on this independent command assignment that would prove to be of great benefit to him later in the war. For the first time in his career he commanded a substantial body of men (25,000) along a broad front (300 miles). Too, he had observed how a railroad could best be used to move large bodies of troops and how it could best be defended.

(Freeman, *op. cit.*, I, 609-30. United States War Department, *The War of the Rebellion: Official Records of the Union and Con-*

federate Armies, (128 vols.; Washington: Government Printing Office, 1880-1901), Series I, Vol. VI, 168-435. This source hereafter will be cited as O. R.)

[38]There was some opposition to the appointment of General Lee to the Southeastern Coast Command. As stated previously, the Richmond papers had ridiculed their fellow Virginian for the manner in which he had conducted the West Virginia Campaign. These stories naturally were picked up and carried by other Southern papers. In view of the opposition, Davis deemed it necessary to advise both Governor Pickens of South Carolina and Governor Brown of Georgia that in his opinion Lee was the best general available for the assignment. Brown, a thorn in Davis' side during the war, assured the President in a letter dated November 7, 1861, that General Lee had his "highest confidence and shall have my cordial cooperation and support."

An unconfirmed story went the rounds at the time of Lee's appointment that nearly all the Confederate and State officers in South Carolina had signed a petition requesting that Lee not be appointed to the command. Davis is reported to have sent word to the petitioners that "if Lee is not a general, I have none that I can send you."

(O. R., *op. cit.,* Series I, Vol. LIII (supl.), 184. Freeman, *op. cit.,* I, 607.)

[39]The Reverend William Meade, the Episcopal rector at Alexandria, Virginia, had drilled Lee in the catechism when the General was a youth. Lee was not confirmed in the Episcopal faith, however, until July 17, 1853. On this date he was confirmed along with two of his daughters (Mary and Annie) by the Right Reverend John Johns, Bishop of Virginia, at the Christ Church in Alexandria.

(Freeman, *op. cit.,* I, 330; II, 251.)

[40]On March 14, 1862, the old rector of Lee's boyhood days, the Right Reverend William Meade, Bishop of Virginia, lay dying. He sent for Lee. Freeman's version of the conversation between the General and the churchman is somewhat different from that of Davis'. According to the Southern historian, the dying bishop said, "God bless you! God bless you, Robert, and fit you for your high and responsible duties. I can't call you 'general'—I must call you 'Robert'; I have heard your Catechism too often."

"Yes, Bishop, very often," said Lee with tears streaming down his cheeks, as he enclosed the bishop's hands in his.

Lee was named to a committee in May, 1868, while he was president of Washington College to plan a memorial for the venerated bishop. Meade had been influential in re-establishing the Protestant Episcopal Church in Virginia following its eclipse after the Revolutionary War.

(Freeman, *op. cit.,* I, 21; IV, 366, 501-02.)

[41]The Battle of Seven Pines, or Fair Oaks, was fought on May 31 and June 1, 1862. The Federal Army was commanded by Major General George B. McClellan and the Confederate Army by General Joseph E. Johnston. This was one of a series of battles fought during McClellan's Peninsular Campaign (April-July, 1862). Both sides had about the same number of men engaged, 42,000. The Confederates lost 6,134 to the Federals' 5,031.

Johnston was seriously wounded in the side and foot during the first day of battle and was succeeded in command by the senior major general on the field, Gustavus Woodson Smith. Smith commanded the army but a few hours. He was succeeded in command by Robert E. Lee early in the afternoon of June 1, 1862. Davis and Lee, who had witnessed the fighting on May 31, rode back to Richmond together that evening. It was during this ride that Davis assigned Lee to command the Confederate Army before Richmond. This was undoubtedly the best and the most important decision that Jefferson Davis made during the war.

(Freeman, *op. cit.,* II, 74. Boatner, *op. cit.,* 272-73. Warner, *Gray, op. cit.,* 280-81.)

[42]Lee, after his return from the southeastern coast in early March, was appointed President Davis' military advisor. "Under the direction of the President," Lee was charged "with the conduct of military operations in the armies of the Confederacy." Thus he had been serving in this thankless but important assignment for three months before assuming the most important field command in the Confederate Army.

(Freeman, *op. cit.,* II, 5.)

[43]Jefferson Davis is referring to the young Quaker teacher, Benjamin Hallowell, who lived next door to the Lees in Alex-

andria. To brush up on his mathematics before entering West Point, Robert E. Lee attended Mr. Hallowell's school during the spring semester of 1825. Hallowell regarded young Lee as "a most exemplary student" who "never failed in a single recitation; was perfectly observant of the rules and regulations of the institution; was gentlemanly, unobtrusive, and respectful in all his deportment to teacher and his fellow students." According to teacher Hallowell, Lee's specialty was "finishing up," and he "imparted a finish and a neatness, as he proceeded, to everything he undertook."

Davis refers to an incident that occurred one day when Lee was working on Conic Sections, a branch of mathematics involving complicated diagrams. Hallowell reported that Lee drew the required diagrams on a slate and "although he well knew that the one he was drawing would have to be removed to make room for another, he drew each one with as much accuracy and finish, lettering and all, as if it were to be engraved and printed."

It is interesting to note that another famous Confederate general, E. Kirby Smith, also attended Benjamin Hallowell's school at Alexandria. Smith attended the school more than a decade after Lee.

(Freeman, *op. cit.*, I, 46-47. Warner, *Gray, op. cit.*, **279.**)

[44]After the Battle of Seven Pines, or Fair Oaks (May 31-June 1, 1862), McClellan shifted his entire army, except for the corps of Fitz John Porter, south of the Chickahominy River near the environs of Richmond. During mid-June the Federal Army was reinforced by some 20,000 effectives bringing McClellan's force to about 91,000. To prevent another Confederate attack such as occurred at Seven Pines, the Union Army entrenched from the Chickahominy to White Oak Swamp, a distance of twelve miles fronting Richmond on the east. The Confederate Army that faced McClellan before Richmond in early June, 1862, numbered not more than 75,000.

(Henry, *op. cit.*, 151-52. Boatner, *op. cit.*, 632-35. Thomas L. Livermore, *Numbers and Losses in the Civil War*, (Bloomington: Indiana University Press, 1957), 140.)

[45]Davis probably had reference to the council of war that Lee had with all the general officers under his command on

June 2, 1862, at "the Chimneys" on the Nine Mile Road near Richmond. The senior generals present were quite perturbed that Lee would discuss a major plan of operations with brigadier generals present.

(Freeman, *op. cit.,* II, 88-89. James Longstreet, *From Manassas to Appomattox,* (Bloomington: Indiana University Press, 1960), 112-13.)

[46]*Boyaus* is a French word meaning narrow passages or trenches. It is unusual to find this French military word in American writings. It is not a common term even among professional soldiers.

[47]Brigadier General W. H. C. "Little Billy" Whiting was the general that provoked Lee's outburst. William Henry Chase Whiting was graduated from West Point as the number one cadet with the Class of 1845. He made the highest grades ever recorded up to that time at the Academy. His record stood until Douglas MacArthur surpassed it in 1903. Whiting was a mathematical genius, hence his "ciphering approach" at Lee's council of war.

Whiting was promoted on the field to brigadier general by President Davis for his outstanding work at First Manassas (July 21, 1861. He commanded a division at Seven Pines (May 31-June 1, 1862) and during the Seven Days' Battles (June 25-(July 1, 1862). After Malvern Hill (July 1, 1862), Whiting was assigned to Wilmington, North Carolina, where he proceeded to build Fort Fisher into the strongest fortress in the Confederacy. He was appointed major general on April 22, 1863. Whiting was given a field command in the summer of 1864 at Petersburg but failed to distinguish himself. Back at Fort Fisher in 1865, Little Billy was severely wounded in the prolonged Federal naval bombardment and the following land assault on January 15. As a prisoner of war he was conveyed to Fort Columbus in New York Harbor, where he died of his wounds on March 10, 1865.

Whiting was a brilliant engineer but failed to produce results as a comamnder of troops in the field.

(Warner, *Gray, op. cit.,* 334-35. Boatner, *op. cit.,* 916.)

[48]To counter the entrenchments dug by the Federals along the Chickahominy facing Richmond, Lee entrenched in a semicircle around the eastern outskirts of the city. Unused to heavy

manual labor and regarding trenches as cowardly and ungentle-
manly, the more caustic Confederate soldiers soon tabbed Lee
the "King of Spades."

(Freeman, op. cit., II, 86-87.)

[49]The Seven Days' Battles were a series of battles fought
during the Peninsular Campaign between June 25 and July 1,
1862. This series of battles consisted of seven independent engagements: Oak Grove (June 25), Mechanicsville (June 26),
Gaines' Mill (June 27), Garnett's and Golding's Farms (June
27-28), Savage's Station (June 29), White Oak Swamp (June
30), and Malvern Hill (July 1).

By this battle or series of engagements Lee drove McClellan
back down the York-James Peninsula to Harrison's Landing on
the James River, where the Federals entrenched. John Pope
succeeded McClellan in command of the Army of the Potomac
during July, 1862. McClellan's troops were then transferred
from the Peninsula to northern Virginia during July and August. The most serious threat to Richmond during 1862 was
over.

Although McClellan was driven from Richmond and soon
afterward from the Peninsula, his retreat was a brilliant military operation. The Federal withdrawal was accomplished
while changing from one base of operations to another—from
White House on the Pamunkey River to Harrison's Landing on
the James. McClellan's successful retreat was assured by the
lack of initiative on the part of several Confederate generals,
particularly Stonewall Jackson.

The only clear-cut Confederate victory during the series of
engagements known collectively as the Seven Days' Battles was
the Battle of Gaines' Mill. Late on the afternoon of June 27
Hood's Texas Brigade broke through the center of Fitz John
Porter's Corps on Turkey Hill above Boatswain's Creek. This
brilliant attack triggered the collapse of the Federal force and
its subsequent retreat across the Chickahominy. Gaines' Mill
was important from another aspect. It was the first engagement for the Army of Northern Virginia as it was finally constituted.

Malvern Hill, the last of the Seven Days' engagements, was
Lee's greatest tactical mistake. His piecemeal attacks against
a strongly prepared position cost the Confederates 5,000 casual-

ties. The Federal loss was scarcely a third of that number.

(Boatner, *op. cit.*, 731-32. Matthew Forney Steele, *American Campaigns*, (2 vols.; Harrisburg: Military Service Publishing Co., 1949), I, 191-216. Harold B. Simpson, *Gaines' Mill to Appomattox*, (Waco: Texian Press, 1963), 83-90.

[50]Lee was restrained both at the battles of The Wilderness (May 5-7, 1864) and Spotsylvania Court House (May 8-18, 1864) from leading units of the Confederate Army into battle. Actually he was stopped on three occasions and not two as Davis stated.

The best known of the "Lee-to-the-rear" episodes occurred during The Wilderness, when the great Virginian attempted to lead Hood's Texas Brigade into battle on May 6. Lee, after praising the Texans for their steadfastness and fighting ability, rode in between the 1st and 4th Texas Regiments, hat in hand, standing in the stirrups, prepared to lead the brigade forward. Several brigades of Hancock's Federal Corps were crashing through the woods toward the Lone Star Brigade but a hundred yards away. At this moment several of the Texans nearest the Confederate commander sprang forward and, surrounding his gray mount, Traveller, grabbed at the reins and saddle trappings in an effort to stay Lee's forward course. Words to the effect of "General Lee to the rear," "We won't move forward until you go back," and "Go back General Lee, go back" were heard on every side. Finally, Colonel Charles Venable of Lee's staff, aided by General John Gregg (commander of the Texans), "forcibly" persuaded the beloved commander to leave the field and join Longstreet, who was directing the disposition of his brigades from a small knoll behind the lines.

Numerous individuals claimed the distinction of staying General Lee's horse—Captain R. J. Harding commanding Company B, 1st Texas and Leonard Groce Gee, Company E, 5th Texas appear to be the heroes. A small monument stands today alongside the Orange Plank Road at the place where Lee attempted to lead the Texans into battle.

The second and third of the "Lee-to-the-rear" episodes occurred during the Battle of Spotsylvania Court House, on May 12, 1864, when Lee was stopped twice on the same day from leading troops into battle. Early in the morning of the twelfth, after the Federals had broken through the Confederate "Mule

Shoe" salient, Lee attempted to lead the 52nd Virginia Infantry Regiment of John Pegram's Brigade and the 13th Georgia Infantry Regiment of John B. Gordon's Brigade into battle to seal off the Federal breakthrough. As at The Wilderness, Traveller was seized and forced back to the cries of "Lee to the rear!" Within an hour or two of this instance, General Lee, in his anxiety to stem the Union advance which had now spread along a wide front, exposed himself recklessly again in an attempt to conduct General Nathaniel H. Harris' Mississippians to the support of Stephan D. Ramseur's Brigade on the Confederate left. Again the cries "Go back, General!! Go back!" were heard on all sides. With the promise from the men that they would drive the Federals from the salient, General Lee retired to a position less exposed to Federal fire.

The Confederate chief came close to losing his life during this latter episode. As he was helping to direct Harris' men along a road toward the breached salient, they came under Federal artillery fire that caused Traveller to rear wildly. After being quieted, the gray mount reared a second time. Just as he did, a solid shot passed just under his girth. Had the horse not reared at that moment, the shot would surely have killed both rider and mount. It was Lee's narrowest escape from death during the war.

(Simpson, *op. cit.,* 202-03. Freeman, *op. cit.,* III, 287-88. Virginia State Historical Society, *Southern Historical Society Papers,* (52 vols.; Richmond, Virginia, 1876-1959), VIII, 107; XIV, 525-26. Listed hereafter as S.H.S.P. Walter H. Taylor, *Four Years With General Lee,* (Bloomington: University of Indiana Press, 1962), 126-27, 207.)

[51]This was the bay stallion Richmond presented to Lee by some of his admirers in the spring of 1861, soon after he had joined the Confederate cause. Richmond died soon after the Battle of Malvern Hill (July 1, 1862).

Besides the famous Traveller, other horses that Lee rode (occasionally) during the war were The Roan, Lucy Long, and Ajax. The Roan went blind early in the war and was given to a Virginia farmer. Traveller, Lucy Long and Ajax accompanied Lee to Lexington after the war. Ajax impaled himself on an iron gate latch and died prior to Lee's death in 1870. Traveller died of lock jaw (June, 1871) soon after the General's death, and his bones were preserved and can be seen today in the Confederate Museum at Richmond. Lucy Long lived until 1891.

(S.H.S.P., *op. cit.*, XIX, 333-34. Freeman, *op. cit.*, I, 644-47. "War Horses of Famous Generals," *Century,* IVXC (May, 1913), 53-54. Laura Spencer Portor and Charles Marshall Graves, "His Love for His Old Gray Horse," *The Ladies' Home Journal,* XXV (January, 1908), 20.)

[52]Lee did not drink, smoke, or curse. Although the Virginian loved good food, particularly fried chicken, game, barbecued shoat, and roast beef, he ate only the simplest of fare while in the field. While the General was the recipient of much fine food donated by residents near his camp or sent long distances by admirers, he was quick to share it with his staff. Often he would distribute the surplus among the soldiers.

Robert E. Lee was very fond of pets. One of his favorites was a small hen that remained a part of his headquarters "paraphernalia" most of the war. She supplied Lee with many a breakfast egg until near the end of the conflict. The pet hen disappeared one day at Petersburg. Undoubtedly, one of the Confederate soldiers succumbed to the pangs of hunger and filched the fowl when she wandered away from the protective influence of General Lee's tent.

(Freeman, *op. cit.,* I, 452. "Haig's Jersey Cows and Lee's Solitary Hen," *Literary Digest,* LXII (August 16, 1919), 56. Burke Davis, *Our Incredible Civil War,* (New York: Holt, Rhinehart & Winston, 1960), 206-07.)

[53]Robert E. Lee, Jr., the youngest son and sixth child of the Robert E. Lees, was born on October 27, 1843, at Arlington, Virginia.

Upon the outbreak of the Civil War, young Lee was a student at the University of Virginia at Charlottesville. He was chosen captain of one of the student companies formed at the university, but upon the advice of his father continued his studies. However, during the winter of 1861-62, Lee enlisted as a private in the Rockbridge Artillery, an elite Virginia battery. This battery was later commanded by Captain W. T. Poague, one of General Lee's favorite officers. Young Lee served with this battery through Jackson's Shenandoah Valley Campaign (May-June, 1862), the Seven Days' Battles (June 25-July 1, 1862) of the Peninsular Campaign (April-July, 1862), and the battles of Second Manassas (August 29-30, 1862), Antietam

(September 16-17, 1862), and Fredericksburg (December 13, 1862). He was promoted to lieutenant in February, 1863, and was assigned as an aide to his older brother, William Henry Fitzhugh "Rooney" Lee, a brigadier general commanding a cavalry brigade under JEB Stuart. Young Robert E. Lee was slightly wounded on August 15, 1864. He was promoted to captain before the end of the war.

Following the war Robert E. Lee, Jr., farmed, first at one of the family estates, White House, and then at Romancoke, an estate left him by his maternal grandfather.

(Freeman, *op. cit.*, I, 190, 511, 605; II, 161, 252, 336, 397, 485; III, 226, 492, 515; IV, 242, 461. O. R., *op. cit.*, Series I, Vol. XI, Part II, 573-74.)

[54]George Washington Custis Lee, the eldest son of Robert E. Lee and the one that most nearly favored his father in looks, was born on September 16, 1832, at Fortress Monroe, Virginia.

He entered the United States Military Academy in 1850 and was graduated number one in the Class of 1854 while his father was superintendent. The Class of 1854 produced several outstanding Civil War generals including Otis O. Howard, John Pegram, JEB Stuart, Archibald Gracie, Stephen Dill Lee (no relation to Custis), and Dorsey Pender.

Custis Lee reluctantly resigned from the United States Army on May 2, 1861. He was appointed a captain of engineers in the Confederate Army and helped to build the fortifications around Richmond. Lee was soon promoted to a colonel of cavalry and served on President Davis' staff from mid-1861 to late 1862. He was promoted to brigadier general June 25, 1863, and to major general on October 20, 1864, although the latter promotion was not confirmed until 1865. Custis served principally as a staff officer during the war, seeing active field duty only during the last few days of the conflict when he accompanied Ewell's Corps on the retreat from Richmond. He was taken prisoner at the Battle of Sayler's Creek (April 6, 1865) but was paroled almost immediately to look after his ailing mother in Richmond.

Following the war Custis Lee taught engineering at Washington College (now Washington and Lee University) at Lexington, Virginia. He succeeded his father as president of the college and served in this capacity for over twenty-five years.

In 1897, Lee took up residence at Ravensworth, where he died on February 18, 1913.

(Warner, *Gray, op. cit.,* 179. *Register of Graduates, op. cit.,* 146. Boatner, *op. cit.,* 475-76.)

[55]Reference footnote number 53.

[56]At the Battle of Antietam (September 16-17, 1862) the Rockbridge Battery lost three of its four guns, sustained several casualties among the cannoneers, and had numerous horses killed.

(Henry, *op. cit.,* 44. O. R., *op. cit.,* Ser. I, Vol. XIX, Part I, 1009-10.)

[57]Robert E. Lee had such few defects of character that his biographers had to look long and hard for an "Achilles heel." Jefferson Davis points out the two "weaknesses" in Lee that most biographers found or parroted from other sources: Lee's habit of suggesting instead of commanding and of treating his contrary subordinates with undue consideration and kindness. Freeman, Lee's greatest biographer, remarked that, "His [Lee's] consideration for others, the virtue of the gentleman, had been his vice as a soldier."

(Freeman, *op. cit.,* IV, 168.)

[58]John Cabell Breckinridge was born near Lexington, Kentucky, on January 15, 1821. He was graduated from Centre College in 1839, afterward attending Transylvania University, where he studied law. Breckinridge fought in the Mexican War (1846-48) and sided with Gideon Pillow in his famous controversy with Winfield Scott. He was practicing law at Lexington, Kentucky, when he was nominated and elected vice-president of the United States on the Buchanan ticket. Breckinridge was only thirty-five at the time. In 1859, a year and a half before his term as vice-president expired, Breckinridge was elected to the senate from Kentucky. Nominated for president on the Southern Democrat ticket, he ran against Lincoln in 1860.

Breckinridge opposed secession but accepted a brigadier general's commission in the Confederate Army on November 2, 1861, after Kentucky declared for the Union the previous September. He was promoted to major general to rank from April

14, 1862. General Breckinridge commanded with gallantry the Reserve Corps at Shiloh (April 6-7, 1862). He further distinguished himself at Murfreesboro or Stone's River (December 31, 1862-January 2, 1863), during the Vicksburg Campaign (May-July, 1863), and at Chickamauga (September 19-20, 1863). He commanded the Department of Southwest Virginia for a short period during 1864 before accompanying Jubal Early on the raid to Washington. On February 4, 1865, Jefferson Davis appointed General Breckinridge Secretary of War. He was the sixth and last man to fill that controversial post in the Confederate cabinet.

During Lee's retreat from Richmond Breckinridge moved south with Davis and the Confederate cabinet. After acting as Joseph E. Johnston's advisor during the surrender negotiations with Sherman, Breckinridge fled to Cuba. He lived for a while in England and then Canada before returning to the United States in 1869. He resumed his law practice at Lexington and was involved in railroad development when he died on May 17, 1875 after a major operation.

(Warner, *Gray*, *op. cit.*, 34-35. Boatner, op. cit., 82-83. *Dictionary of American Biography, op. cit.*, II, 7-10.)

[59]Isaac Munroe St. John was born at Augusta, Georgia, on November 19, 1827. He was graduated from Yale University in 1845. During the next three years St. John studied law in New York City, edited a newspaper in Baltimore, and served as a civil engineer with the Baltimore and Ohio Railroad. From 1855 to 1861 he served as an engineer with the Blue Ridge Railroad in Georgia and South Carolina.

After the firing on Fort Sumter, St. John enlisted as a private in a South Carolina company known as the "Fort Hill Guards." He was commissioned a captain of engineers during the fall of 1861 and served as "Prince John" Magruder's engineering officer at Yorktown. As a major he was placed in charge of the Nitre Corps (later Nitre and Mining Corps) in October, 1862. St. John was eventually promoted to colonel as head of the Nitre Corps and rendered invaluable service to the Confederacy. On February 16, 1865, by special act of the Confederate Congress, St. John was promoted to brigadier general and replaced the harried Lucius B. Northrop as commissary general.

Following the war General St. John served in various civil engineering capacities. He was with several Southern railroads first and then for two years served as the chief engineer for the City of Louisville. At the time of his death in 1880, St. John was a consulting engineer with the Chesapeake and Ohio Railroad and chief engineer of the Elizabeth, Lexington, and Big Sandy Railroad.

(Warner, *Gray, op. cit.,* 267-68.. Boatner, *op. cit.,* 716-17. *Dictionary of American Biography, op. cit.,* VIII, 302-03.)

[60]Louis E. Harvie, president of the Richmond and Danville Railroad, was one of the few men of the time who fully realized the value of the iron horse as a military weapon. Early in the war he urged the creation of an inter-line freight car pool among the Southern railroads. Unfortunately for the South, this intelligent proposal was not adopted and thus the Confederacy had little flexibility in its railroad system. At Harvie's insistence, the Confederate Congress finally built the Piedmont Railroad (1862-64) linking the Richmond and Danville with the North Carolina Railroad, thus giving Richmond direct access to the rich agricultural area of western North Carolina.

(Robert C. Black III, *The Railroads of the Confederacy,* (Chapel Hill: University of North Carolina Press, 1952), 29, 69, 75-77.)

[61]The Richmond and Danville Railroad ran from Richmond, Virginia, through Burkeville (where it crossed the South Side Railroad) to Danville, Virginia. At Danville it linked (in 1864) with the Piedmont Railroad that ran to Greensboro, North Carolina, and joined the North Carolina Railroad.

The Richmond and Danville Railroad, one of the most important railroads to the Confederacy, was built on a five-foot gauge in the 1850's. It was one of the few Southern railroads that had an organized telegraph department to allow flexibility in traffic control and scheduling.

The R & D ran the last train out of Richmond on April 3, carrying Jefferson Davis and the remnants of the Confederate government from the burning capital.

(Black, *op. cit.,* endsheet (railroad map), 13, 24, 35, 282, 285-86.)

[62]Freeman in his definitive work on General Lee devotes five pages of discussion to this subject (Appendix IV-2, pp. 509-13).

It appears that from an analysis of the sources that Freeman quotes and from his own remarks, Lee did not specifically
request by written order that the supplies, concentrated at Danville for the army, be sent to Amelia Court House, the designated concentration point for the Confederate divisions streaming west from Richmond and Petersburg. Delays in the trans-
mission of several important orders relating to the transportation of supplies further cloud the issue and complicate the analysis of the testimony given by the interested parties. The fact
that the railroad cars were all reserved to carry Confederate
government personnel, archives, and bullion from Richmond
makes the political hierarchy of the government appear to be
the culprits in the affair—the diverting of the transportation
that was needed to bring food and supplies to Lee's Army.

Colonel W. H. Taylor, Lee's Assistant Adjutant General,
writing many years after the war, asserted that to his knowledge no specific order was given by General Lee asking that
supplies be sent to Amelia Court House. However, it was Taylor's opinion that Lee's second telegram on April 2 to the Secretary of War stating that he was directing all of his troops to
Amelia Court House should have been order enough that the
supplies and food be sent there. Where else would an intelligent,
reasonable staff officer send supplies but to where the army was
concentrating, Taylor asked. Taylor added that Lee, in his own
mind "thought that he had given all orders necessary and expected to find supplies at Amelia Court House." As soon as
Lee's first telegram of April 2 stating that he would concentrate
"near the Danville Railroad [Richmond and Danville]" became
known in Richmond, the Confederate commissary general, Brigadier General I. M. St. John, wired Colonel R. G. Cole, Lee's
chief commissary, asking to what destination the reserve rations
then in Richmond should be sent. This inquiry never reached
Colonel Cole. However, St. John, not receiving a reply, requi-
sitioned every wheeled vehicle possible and sent the 350,000 rations of bread and meat after Lee's retreating army. The Federal Army, into whose hands the victuals finally fell, having
ample food supplies of their own, largely ignored the rancid
rations.

It is easy to see how a misunderstanding such as this could
have occurred. The Confederacy was in a state of collapse, telegraph lines were down, the railroad schedules were confused

or non-existent, available rolling stock was insufficient to meet the conflicting emergency needs, and the army and the government were on the move. It is difficult if not impossible to assess the blame for food and supplies not being at Amelia Court House when Lee's Army arrived there on April 4, 1865.

(S.H.S.P., *op. cit.*, III, 97-103.)

[63]One of the bitterest controversies stemming from the Civil War concerned Longstreet's failure to attack Little Round Top early on the morning of July 2, 1863, at Gettysburg.

During the evening of July 1, Lee held a conference of his corps commanders (with key staff members also in attendance) and informed them (over Longstreet's misgivings) that he planned to attack the Union position the next morning. The time that Lee set for the attack on the second is not clear. Inasmuch as this was one of the major points in the dispute that erupted after the war, the time of attack was given quite a public hearing by the anti-Longstreet faction. General A. L. Long of Lee's staff remembered Lee saying, "Gentlemen we shall attack the enemy as early as practicable." Others in attendance at the meeting "remembered" many years after the war that Lee had given Longstreet specific orders to attack early. Longstreet in his war memoirs *(From Manassas to Appomattox)* denies this, saying that "General Lee never in his life gave me orders to attack at a specific hour. He was perfectly satisfied that when I had my troops in position and was ordered to attack, no time was ever lost. On the night of the first [July 1, 1863], I left him [Lee] without any orders at all."

It is a known fact that Lee seldom gave written attack orders or even specific verbal orders. He was in the habit of outlining his general plan of attack and then letting his lieutenants fight the battle within this framework under his general guidance.

Actually all of the Union corps were up and in position on Cemetery Ridge by 9:00 a.m. on July 2, except John Sedgwick's 6th Corps. At 9:00 a.m. Lee was still making his attack arrangements. Inasmuch as the Union Army was in position early, the only advantage left to Lee, who was committed to taking the offensive, was to keep the place and exact time of his attack secret and thus use the element of surprise as his key to victory.

It was a known fact that Longstreet wanted to fight a defensive battle at Gettysburg. If the Confederates must take the offensive, he said, they should outflank the Federal left—go south of Little Round Top, turn the Union flank, and destroy the wagon trains huddled behind Cemetery Hill and force Meade from his strong position. Lee, however, had ordered the attack up the Emmitsburg Pike and thus would hit the Union left wing at the oblique. Longstreet offered several excuses for not attacking. Two of his important units were not up—Law's Brigade of Hood's Division and Pickett's Division. Lee gave permission to wait for Law but not for Pickett. Finally, after Law's Brigade joined and after meandering several miles through the woods behind the Confederate right (to avoid detection), Longstreet's Corps smashed into the Union left at about 4:00 p.m. on July 2. Although driving in Sickles' exposed corps and fighting his way brilliantly through Devil's Den, Longstreet failed to take Little Round Top—the key to the Federal position. Just prior to Longstreet's troops reaching this important objective, Meade (thanks to General G. K. Warren) fortified the hill with infantry and artillery, thus thwarting the attack by the tired Texans and Alabamians.

The actual controversy over who was to blame for the Confederate defeat at Gettysburg did not develop until after Lee's death. Too, it wasn't until about ten years after the battle that Gettysburg was first seen in its true light as being the turning point of the war.

Lee, who was not addicted to criticizing his subordinates, mentioned only in his final report of the battle "that General Longstreet's dispositions [on July 2] were not completed as early as expected." This seemingly innocent remark, long after it was made, was pounced upon as one of the major reasons for the loss at Gettysburg, given much publicity, and the spark of controversy was fanned to a bright flame. The spark fanner was General S. N. Pendleton, Chief of Artillery of the Army of Northern Virginia, who started the controversy during a lecture tour that he embarked on in 1872. Pendleton stated unequivocally that "General Longstreet had been ordered by Lee on the night of July 1, before he went back to his headquarters toward Cashtown, to attack the Federal left at sunrise on July 2 and that he failed to do this, which brought about the defeat of the Southern forces."

General Pendleton's accusation set off a quarrel between

several of Lee's staff officers and "Old Pete" and his adherents. Longstreet lost favor in the South after the war when he embraced the Republican party and the Catholic faith and thus fought a losing battle as far as the Southern public was concerned. Too, Lee was more venerable in death than he had been in life, and his admirers were determined that the loss of what now appeared to be the crucial battle of the war would not rest on General Lee's shoulders.

The Lee-Longstreet-Gettysburg controversy is still active or at least was up until a few years ago (1950's), when two of the outstanding writers in the field of Civil War history took opposite sides on the question. Douglas Southall Freeman, as could be expected, defended Lee's actions on July 2 and Kenneth P. Williams supported Longstreet's contentions.

But why blame any Confederate general—Lee, Longstreet, Ewell, or Stuart—for the Southern defeat at Gettysburg? The Federal Army of the Potomac fought its best fight to date at Gettysburg. Under the leadership of dour but dogged George Gordon Meade, the Federals fought with skill, persistence, and bravery, and tenaciously defended on July 2 and 3, 1863, a position of natural strength. The Union Army in the East had found itself at last, and to it should go the credit for Lee's defeat—not to one or a combination of Confederate generals.

(Harold B. Simpson, *Brawling Brass: North and South*, (Waco: Texian Press, 1961), 29-39. Longstreet, *op. cit.*, 362-408. A. L. Long, *Memoirs of Robert E. Lee*, (New York: J. M. Stoddart and Co., 1886), 276-88. O. R., *op. cit.*, Series I, Vol. XXVII, 313-25.)

[64]After driving the Federal Army through Gettysburg and on to a defensive position on Cemetery Ridge south of the town on July 1, Lee decided to test both of the Federal flanks on the second. However, Ewell failed on the Confederate left at Culp's Hill and Longstreet failed on the Confederate right at Little Round Top on that memorable second day of battle. On the third day Lee, supposing that the Federal center had been weakened to support both of the flanks which had been hit the previous day, determined to smash through Hancock's superb II Corps defending the center of Meade's well-balanced line.

Pickett's Division of Longstreet's Corps was selected to spearhead the attack against the Union center. George Pickett's men had not come up from Chambersburg in time to be engaged on July 2 with the rest of Longstreet's Corps so his

division was fresh. To support Pickett's Virginians, Lee selected Pettigrew's North Carolina Division that had seen much action on July 1 but little on July 2. An artillery barrage of some
170 guns preceded the Confederate attack. Longstreet, who
was opposed to Lee's plan to attack the Federal center, reluctantly authorized the Confederate infantry to move forward
after the abbreviated artillery barrage had subsided. "Pickett's Charge" failed—the Union center bent but did not break;
superior Union artillery and massed blue infantry were awaiting
the expected Southern attack. The Confederates lost over 50
per cent of their 8,000-man attacking force.

 [65]As the bloody survivors of the Confederate attack against
the Union center on July 3 came streaming back toward Sem-
inary Ridge, they were met by a sorrowful General Lee. Pickett,
beset with grief at the loss of his brigade commanders and a
greater part of his division, was told by Lee: "This has been
my fight and upon my shoulders rests the blame. The men and
officers of your command have written the name of Virginia as
high today as it has ever been written before." As the Virginians continued passing to the rear Lee remarked to Pickett
again: "your men have done all that men could do; the fault is
entirely my own."

 To General Cadmus Wilcox, General Lee directed the remark that Jefferson Davis probably had reference to. Wilcox,
in a battered straw hat, passed Lee soon after Pickett had talked
to the commander. Wilcox's Brigade had suffered heavy losses,
and the Tennesseean was filled with emotion as he attempted
to explain the condition of his troops. Lee grasped his hand
saying: "Never mind, General; all this has been my fault—it is
I who have lost this fight, and you must help me out of it the
best way you can."

(S.H.S.P., *op. cit.*, XXXI, 233-35. James A. L. Fremantle, *The
Fremantle Diary*, (Boston: Little, Brown, and Co., 1954), 215-16.)

 [66]Davis was captured near Irwinsville, Georgia, on May 10,
1865, as he fled toward Texas. He was imprisoned at Fortress
Monroe for two years. In 1867, Davis was released by writ of
habeas corpus and brought before the Federal circuit court at
Richmond for trial on a charge of treason. The Federal attor-
neys were not ready to present their case and the ex-Confeder-
ate President was released on a $100,000 bond. Two of the men

who provided bond for Davis were Cornelius Vanderbilt and Horace Greeley, editor of the New York *Tribune.* Davis' trial had many legal complications and was constantly delayed. Finally prosecution was dropped after President Johnson's proclamation of unconditional amnesty on Christmas Day, 1868.

Lee surrendered the Army of Northern Virginia to General U. S. Grant at the McLean House in the town of Appomattox Court House, Virginia, on the afternoon of April 9, 1865. Sometime before April 12, probably during the afternoon of April 11, General Lee along with his staff officers signed the general parole required by the terms of the surrender. Lee signed the individual parole of Colonel W. H. Taylor, the only parole document which required the Confederate commander's signature. Taylor, as the assistant adjutant general, signed the individual paroles of Lee's other staff officers and of General Lee himself. The Army of Northern Virginia, as a whole, was formally paroled on April 12, 1865.

(Walter H. Taylor, *General Lee: His Campaign in Virginia, 1861-1865, With Personal Reminiscences,* (Norfolk, Virginia, 1906), 296.)

[67]According to Professor J. T. Dorris, the outstanding authority on amnesty and pardon of the Confederate leaders, an attempt was made soon after the war to arrest General Lee and indict him for treason regardless of his being paroled by Grant. Lee immediately appealed to Grant, who protested to President Johnson on the Virginian's behalf. When the President permitted the indictment proceedings to continue, Grant threatened to resign as commander in chief of the Federal Army. Convinced of Grant's earnestness, Johnson gave in, and the indictment was dropped and the proceedings were stopped.

It is interesting to note that Lee's application for pardon or amnesty was a simple request of fewer than one hundred words. John Reagan's, Alexander Stephens', and Christopher Memminger's requests for pardon contained 2,500 words or more each.

(J. T. Dorris, "Pardoning the Leaders of the Confederacy," *The Mississippi Valley Historical Review,* (June, 1928), Vol. XV, 6-7.)

Appendix
Selected Bibliography
and
Index

EDITOR'S NOTE

After the Battle of Gettysburg Lee was depressed by the tremendous number of casualties (about 23,000) suffered by the Confederate Army during the engagement. The underlying cause for the failure of the campaign, Lee said, was due primarily to the lack of coordination, thus overlooking all of the tactical errors of his subordinates and shouldering the blame for the setback himself. Lee admitted he had expected too much from his army and that his overconfidence had carried him too far. Too, Lee had not felt well during the spring and early summer of 1863, suffering at various times from neuralgia and diarrhea.

Depressed and dejected by this series of emotional and physical setbacks General Lee asked of the President to be relieved as commander of the Army of Northern Virginia. Thus the stage was set for the exchange of letters in early August, 1863, between Lee and Davis on the subject of the former's resignation. The cordial wartime relationship that existed between the two Confederate leaders is nowhere better illustrated than in these two letters.

* * * * *

Camp Orange
August 8, 1863

His Excellency JEFFERSON DAVIS,
President of the Confederate States:

Mr. President: Your letters of July 28 and August 2 have been received, and I have waited for a leisure hour to reply, but I fear that will never come. I am extremely obliged to you for the attention given to the wants of this army, and the efforts made to supply them. Our absentees are returning, and I hope the earnest and beautiful appeal made to the country in your proclamation may stir up the virtue of the whole people, and that they may see their duty and perform it. Nothing is wanted but that their fortitude should equal their bravery to insure the success of our cause. We must expect reverses, even defeats. They are sent to teach us wisdom and prudence, to call forth greater energies, and to prevent our falling into greater disasters. Our people have only to be true and united, to bear manfully the misfortunes incident to war, and all will come right in the end.

I know how prone we are to censure and how ready to blame others for the non-fulfillment of our expectations. This is unbecoming in a generous people, and I grieve to see its expression. The general remedy for the want of success in a military commander is his removal. This is natural, and, in many instances proper. For, no matter what may be the ability of the officer, if he loses the confidence of his troops disaster must sooner or later ensue.

I have been prompted by these reflections more than once since my return from Pennsylvania to propose to your Excellency the propriety of selecting another commander for this army. I have seen and heard of expression of discontent in the public journals at the result of the expedition. I do not know how far this feeling extends in the army. My brother officers have been too generous to exhibit it. It is fair, however, to suppose that it does exist, and success is so necessary to us that nothing should be risked to secure it. I therefore, in all sincerity, request Your Excellency to take measures to supply my place. I do this with the more earnestness because no one is more aware than myself of my inability for the duties of my position. I cannot even accomplish what I myself desire. How can I fulfill the expectations of others? In addition I sensibly feel the growing failure of my bodily strength. I have not yet recovered from the attack I experienced the past spring. I am becoming more and more incapable of exertion, and am thus prevented from making the personal examinations in the field and giving the personal supervision to the operations in the field which I feel to be necessary. I am so dull that in making use of the eyes of others I am frequently misled. Everything, therefore, points to the advantages to be derived from a new commander, and I the more anxiously urge the matter upon Your Excellency from my belief that a younger and abler man than myself can readily be attained. I know that he will have as gallant and brave an army as ever existed to second his efforts, and it would be the happiest day of my life to see at its head a worthy leader—one that would accomplish more than I could perform and all that I have wished. I hope Your Excellency will attribute my request to the true reason, the desire to serve my country, and to do all in my power to insure the success of her righteous cause.

I have no complaints to make of any one but myself. I have received nothing but kindness from those above me, and the most considerate attention from my comrades and companions in arms. To Your Excellency I am especially indebted for uniform kindness and consideration. You have done everything in your power to aid me in the work committed to my charge, without omitting anything to promote the general welfare. I pray that your efforts may at length be crowned with success, and that you may long live to enjoy the thanks of a grateful people.

With sentiments of great esteem, I am, very respectfully and truly, yours,

R. E. LEE
General

Richmond, Va.
August 11, 1863

General R. E. LEE,
Commanding Army of Northern Virginia:
Yours of 8th instant has been received. I am glad that you concur so entirely with me as to the want of our country in this trying hour, and am happy to add that after the first depres-

sion consequent upon our disaster in the west, indications have appeared that our people will exhibit that fortitude which we agree in believing is alone needful to secure ultimate success.

It well became Sidney Johnston, when overwhelmed by a senseless clamor, to admit the rule that success is the test of merit; and yet there has been nothing which I have found to require a greater effort of patience than to bear the criticisms of the ignorant, who pronounce everything a failure which does not equal their expectations or desires, and can see no good result which is not in the line of their own imaginings. I admit the propriety of your conclusions, that an officer who loses the confidence of his troops should have his position changed, whatever may be his ability, but when I read the sentence I was not at all prepared for the application you were about to make. Expressions of discontent in the public journals furnished but little evidence of the sentiment of an army. I wish it were otherwise, even though all the abuse of myself should be accepted as the results of honest observation. I say I wish I could feel that the public journals were not generally partisan nor venal.

Were you capable of stooping to it, you could easily surround yourself with those who would fill the press with your laudations, and seek to exalt you for what you had not done, rather than detract from the achievements which will make you and your army the subject of history and object of the world's admiration for generations to come.

I am truly sorry to know that you still feel the effects of the illness you suffered last spring, and can readily understand the embarrassments you experience in using the eyes of others, having been so much accustomed to make your own reconnaissances. Practice will, however, do much to relieve that embarrassment, and the minute knowledge of the country which you have acquired will render you less dependent for topographical information.

But suppose, my dear friend, that I were to admit, with all their implications, the points which you present, where am I to find that new commander who is to possess the greater abliity which you believe to be required? I do not doubt the readiness with which you would give way to one who could accomplish all that you have wished, and you will do me the justice to believe that if Providence should kindly offer such a person for our use, I would not hesitate to avail of his services.

My sight is not sufficiently penetrating to discover such hidden merit, if it exists, and I have but used to you the language of sober earnestness when I have impressed upon you the propriety of avoiding all unnecessary exposure to danger, because I felt our country could not bear to lose you. To ask me to substitute you by some one in my judgment more fit to command, or who would possess more of the confidence of the army, or of the reflecting men of the country, is to demand an impossibility.

It only remains for me to hope that you will take all possible care of yourself, that your health and strength may be entirely restored, and that the Lord will preserve you for the important duties devolved upon you in the struggle of our suffering country for the independence which we have engaged in war to maintain.

As ever, very respectfully and truly, yours,

JEFFERSON DAVIS.

SELECTED BIBLIOGRAPHY

Primary Sources

Fremantle, James A. L., *The Fremantle Diary*, Boston: Little Brown and Co., 1954 (reprint).

Headquarters, Department of Texas, Special Order No. 136, dated October 21, 1857, Records of the Department of Texas, National Archives, Washington, D.C.

Long, A. L., *Memoirs of Robert E. Lee*, New York: J. M. Stoddart and Co., 1886.

Longstreet, James, *From Manassas to Appomattox*, Bloomington: Indiana University Press, 1960 (reprint).

Post Returns for Fort Mason, Texas, 1857-1861, Records of the Department of Texas, National Archives, Washington, D.C.

Rapp, Kenneth W., letters dated December 7, 1965, and May 20, 1966.

Taylor, Walter, *Four Years With General Lee*, Bloomington: University of Indiana Press, 1962 (reprint).

.... *General Lee: His Campaign in Virginia, 1861-1865, With Personal Reminiscences*, Norfolk, Virginia, 1906.

United States War Department, *The War of the Rebellion: Official Records of the Union and Confederate Armies*, 128 vols., Washington: Government Printing Office, 1880-1901.

Virginia State Historical Society, *Southern Historical Society Papers*, 52 vols., Richmond, Virginia, 1876-1959.

Secondary Sources

Bill, Alfred Hoyt, *Rehearsal for Conflict*, New York: Alfred A. Knopf, 1947.

Black, Robert C. III, *The Railroads of the Confederacy*, Chapel Hill: University of North Carolina Press, 1952.

Boatner, Mark M. III, *The Civil War Dictionary*, New York: David McKay Co., 1959.

Crane, John and James F. Keiley, *West Point, Key to America*, New York: McGraw, Hill Book Co., 1947.

Davis, Burke, *Our Incredible Civil War*, New York: Holt, Rhinehart and Winston, 1960.

Dictionary of American Biography, Dumas Malone (ed.), 11 vols., New York: Charles Scribner's Sons, 1961.

Dictionary of American History, James Truslow Adams (ed.), 4 vols., New York: Charles Scribner's Sons, 1940.

Dorris, J. T., "Pardoning the Leaders of the Confederacy," *The Mississippi Valley Review*, Vol. 15 (June, 1928).

Freeman, Douglas Southall, *R. E. Lee*, 4 vols., New York: Charles Scribner's Sons, 1934.

Green, Laurence, *The Raid*, New York: Henry Holt and Company, 1953.

"Haig's Jersey Cows and Lee's Solitary Hen," *Literary Digest,* Vol. 62 (August 16, 1919).

Heitman, Francis B., *Historical Register and Dictionary of the United States Army,* 2 vols., Washington: Government Printing Office, 1903.

Henry, Robert Selph, *The Mexican War,* Indianapolis: Bobbs, Merrill Co., 1950.

————, *The Story of the Confederacy,* New York: Grosset and Dunlap, 1936.

Herr, John K. and Edward S. Wallace, *The Story of the United States Cavalry, 1775-1942,* Boston: Little, Brown and Co., 1953.

Johnson, Richard W., *A Soldier's Reminiscences in Peace and War,* Philadelphia: J. B. Lippincott Co., 1886.

Livermore, Thomas L., *Numbers and Losses in the Civil War,* Bloomington: Indiana University Press, 1957 (reprint).

Portor, Laura Spencer and Charles Marshall Graves, "His Love for His Old Gray Horse," *The Ladies' Home Journal,* Vol. 25 (January, 1908).

Price, George F., *Across the Continent With the Fifth Cavalry,* New York: Antiquarian Press, Ltd., 1959.

Register of Graduates and Former Cadets of the United States Military Academy, New York: West Point Alumni Foundation, Inc., 1964.

Rister, Carl Coke, *Robert E. Lee in Texas,* Norman: University of Oklahoma Press, 1946.

Simpson, Harold B., *Brawling Brass—North and South,* Waco: Texian Press, 1961.

————, *From Gaines' Mill to Appomattox,* Waco: Texian Press, 1963.

Spaulding, Oliver L., *The United States Army in War and Peace,* New York: G. P. Putnam's Sons, 1937.

Steele, Matthew Forney, *American Campaigns,* Harrisburg: Military Service Publishing Co., 1949 (reprint).

Sterling, Carlos Marquez, *Historia de Cuba,* New York: Las Americas Publishing Co., 1963.

Strode, Hudson, *Jefferson Davis, American Patriot,* New York: Harcourt, Brace and Co., 1955.

The West Point Atlas of American Wars, Vincent J. Esposito (chief ed.), 2 vols., New York: Frederick A. Praeger, 1959.

Warner, Ezra J., *Generals in Gray,* Baton Rouge: Louisiana State University Press, 1959.

————, *Generals in Blue,* Baton Rouge: Louisiana State University Press, 1964.

Index

— A —

Amelia, Court House, 10, 11, 62-63
Anaconda Plan, 24
Arista, General Mariano, 22
Army of Northern Virginia, 25, 54, 67
Army of Observation, 19
Army of Tennessee, 45
Army of the Center, 18, 20
Army of the Rio Grande, 22
Army of the West, 19
Army of Utah, 36
Army of Virginia, 8
Antietam, Battle of (See Sharpsburg)
Ajax (Lee's horse), 56
Atlanta Campaign, 45

— B —

Babcock, Major Samuel, 17
Baltimore and Ohio Railroad, 46, 60
Barnard, Bvt. Major Jonathan G., 33
Beauregard, Fort (So. Car.), 48
Beauregard, General G. T. P., 26, 44
Belen Gate, Battle of, 28
Benton, Senator Thomas Hart, 34
Blackhawk, Chief, 21
Blackhawk War, 21, 23, 27
Blair, Montgomery, Sr., 40-41
Bland's (Theodorick) Regiment, 13
Blue Ridge Railroad, 60
Bragg, General Braxton, 25, 45
Brazos de Santiago (Texas), 22, 24
Breckinridge, General John C., 10, 59-60
Brewerton, Captain Henry, 33
Bridger, Fort, 36
Brown, John, 37-38

Brown, Governor Joseph E., 48, 50
Buchanan, President, James, 24, 32, 35, 37
Buena Vista, Battle of, 2, 19, 22, 25

— C —

Cadwalader, General George, 2, 26, 29
Calhoun, Fort (Va.), 17
Calhoun, John C., 16, 33
Cameron, Simon, 40-42
Carnifix Ferry, Battle of, 47
Carrick's Ford, Battle of, 46
Carroll, Charles, 30
Carroll, Fort (Maryland), 3, 30
Caswell, Fort (North Carolina), 17-18
Cerro Gordo, Battle of, 23, 27, 29, 44
Céspedes, Carlos Manuel de, 31
Chapultepec, Battle of, 23, 28-30
Cheat Mountain (West Virginia), 6
Chesapeake and Ohio Railroad, 61
Chickamauga, Battle of, 60
Chippewa, Battle of, 23
Churubusco, Battle of, 23, 26, 28, 30
Cleveland, President Grover, 45
Cockspur Island (Ga.), 17
Cole, Colonel R. G., 62
Colorado, Camp (Tex.), 39
Columbus, Fort (N.Y.), 53
Contreras, Battle of, 2, 23, 25, 28-30
Cooper, Camp (Tex.), 39
Cooper, General Samuel, 44
Cortinas, Juan, 39
Cosby, General George B., 35
Creole (Lee's horse), 25
Crittenden, John J., 31
Crittenden, William, 31

Cross Keys, Battle of (See Port Republic)
Custis, G. W. P., 36

— D —

Davis, Jefferson
Released on bond after the Civil War, 12; Cadet at the United States Military Academy, 14-15; Takes custody of Chief Blackhawk, 21; At Buena Vista, 25; Asked to command expedition to Cuba, 31; Improvements made as Secretary of War, 32; Success as Secretary of War, 33; Helps to organize the 2nd U. S. Cavalry Regt., 34; Relieves Joseph E. Johnston of command at Atlanta, 45; Feuds with Joseph E. Johnston, 45; Directs the fortification of the southeastern coast, 48; Supports Lee as commander of the Southeastern Coast Command, 50; Promotes W. H. C. Whiting to general, 53; G. W. Custis Lee serves on staff, 58; Appoints Breckinridge Secretary of War, 60; Captured near Irwinsville, Georgia, 66; Imprisoned at Fort Monroe, 66-67; Defended by Lee before the grand jury, 11; Charges dropped, 67
Donelson, Fort (Tenn)., 49
Du Pont, Admiral Samuel, 48
Dorris, Professor J. T., 67

— E —

Early, General Jubal, 60
11th U. S. Infantry Regiment, 29
Elizabeth, Lexington and Big Sandy Railroad, 61
Eutaw Springs, Battle of, 13
Evans, General Nathan "Shanks," 35

Ewell, General Richard, 58, 65

— F —

Field, General Charles W., 35
5th U. S. Infantry Regiment, 36
52nd Virginia Infantry Regiment, 56
Fillmore, President Millard, 31-32
1st Texas Infantry Regiment, 55
1st U. S. Artillery, 28
1st U. S. Cavalry Regiment, 34, 40
1st U. S. Infantry Regiment, 21
Fish, Hamilton, 31
Fisher, Fort (No. Caro.), 53
Floyd, General John, 24, 56
Ford, Governor Thomas, 27
Fort Hill Guards, 60
14th U. S. Infantry Regiment, 29
4th Texas Infantry Regiment, 55
4th U. S. Artillery, 36
4th U. S. Infantry Regiment, 21
Fraser, Captain William D., 20
Fredericksburg, Battle of, 58
Freeman, Douglas Southall, 65
Fremont, General John C., 19

— G —

Gaines' Mill, Battle of, 54
García, ..., 31
Garnett's and Golding's Farms, Battle of, 54
Garnett, General Robert S., 33, 46
Garrard, General Kenner, 35
Gee, Leonard Groce, 55
Gettysburg, Battle of, 11
Gómez, ..., 31
Gordon, General John B., 56
Grant, General Ulysses S., 9, 11, 31, 45, 67
Gracie, General Archibald, 33, 58

Gratiot, General Charles I., 17
Greeley, Horace, 67
Green, Lieutenant Israel, 37-38
Greene, General Nathaniel, 13-14
Gregg, General John, 55
Guiliford Court House, Battle of, 13

— H —

Halleck, General Henry W., 19
Hallowell, Benjamin, 51
Hamilton, Fort (N.Y.), 18
Hampton, General Wade, 23
Hardee, General William J., 35
Harding, Captain R. J., 55
Harris, General Nathaniel H., 56
Harrison, General William Henry, 21
Harvie, Louis E., 11, 61
Henry, Fort (Tenn.), 49
Hood, General John Bell, 33, 35, 45, 64
Hood's Texas Brigade, 54-55
Houston, Senator Sam, 34
Howard, General Oliver Otis, 33, 58

— J —

Jackson, General Stonewall, 54
Jefferson, President Thomas, 24
Jessup, Fort (La.), 21-22
John Brown's Raid, 4, 37-38
Johns, Bishop John, 50
Johnson, President Andrew, 67
Johnson, General Richard W., 35, 39
Johnston, General Albert Sidney, 3, 34-36, 44
Johnston, General Joseph E., 6, 44-45, 51, 60

— K —

Kearney, General Stephen W., 19

Knights of the Golden Circle, 39
Knox, Fort (Ky.), 21

— L —

Law, General Evander, 64
Leavenworth, Fort, 19, 29, 36
Lee, Annie, 50
Lee, General Charles, 9
Lee, General Fitzhugh, 33, 35
Lee, General G. W. Custis, 10, 33, 58-59
Lee, Henry (Light Horse Harry), 1, 3, 13-14
Lee, John, 40
Lee's Legion (Revolutionary War), 13
Lee, Mary, 50
Lee, General Robert Edward
Birthplace, 1; Enters West Point, 1, 16; Record as a cadet, 1, 16; Commissioned in the Corps of Engineers, 16-17; Assigned to Cockspur Island (Georgia), 17; Assigned to Old Point Comfort (Virginia), 17; Promoted to second lieutenant, 17; Assigned to staff of General Charles I. Gratiot, 17; Surveys disputed boundary between states of Michigan and Ohio, 17; Promoted to first lieutenant, 17; Assigned to St. Louis engineering project, 17; Promoted to captain, 17; Promotions in the Corps of Engineers, 1; Assigned to duty inspecting East Coast forts, 17; Assigned to Fort Hamilton (New York), 18; Member of West Point Examining Board, 18; Assigned to office of Chief of Engineers, 18; Member of Board of Engineers for the Atlantic Coast Defense, 18; Joins Wool's Army at San Antonio, 19; marches with

Wool's Army into Mexico, 20; Transfers to Scott's Army at Brazos de Santiago, 2, 25; At the Battle of Contreras, 2, 25-26; Brevet promotions during Mexican War, 29-30; Assigned to Fort Carroll project, 3, 30; Asked to command expedition to Cuba, 3, 31; Appointed Superintendent of West Point, 3, 33; Appointed lieutenant colonel of the 2nd U. S. Cavalry Regiment, 3, 34-35; Takes command of the 2nd Cavalry, 36-37; Returns to Virginia to settle father-in-law's estate, 37; Ordered to Harper's Ferry, 4, 36-38; Returns to Texas as department commander, 38-39; Plan to defend Fort Mason, 39; Leaves Texas, 40; Resigns from the United States Army, 4, 41-42; Takes command of Virginia state forces, 5, 42; Loyalty discussed, 43-44; Ranking as a Confederate general, 44, 46; Commands in Western Virginia, 6, 45-47; Criticized for efforts in Western Virginia, 7, 47-48; Assigned to the Southeastern Coast Command, 7, 10, 48-49; At Bishop Meade's death, 7, 50-51; Takes command of the Confederate Army in Virginia, 8, 51; Provoked by General W. H. C. Whiting, 8-9, 53; Entrenches around Richmond, 53-54; Exposes self to enemy fire, 9, 55-56; Almost killed, 56; Simple fare and habits, 9-10, 57; Careful not to hurt feelings of others, 9, 59; Sense of humor, 9; Meets son Robbie at Sharpsburg, 10; Greets lady who gave him bread, 10; Controversy over non-receipt of supplies at Amelia Court House, 10-11, 62-63; Generalship at Gettysburg, 11; Lee-Longstreet controversy, 63-65; Takes blame for loss of battle, 65-66; Paroled after Appomattox, 11, 67; Indicted for treason, 67; Defends Davis before the grand jury, 11; Negro juror sleeps during Lee's testimony, 12

Lee, Mrs. Robert E., 37-38
Lee, Robert E., Jr., 10, 57-58
Lee, General Stephen Dill, 33, 58
Lee, General William H. Fitzhugh "Rooney," 58
Lincoln, President Abraham, 24, 27, 40
Long, General A. L., 63
Longstreet, General Pete, 55, 63-65
Lopez, Narcisco, 30
Loring, General W. W. "Blizzards," 46
Lucy Long (Lee's horse), 56-57
Lundy's Lane, Battle of, 23

— M —

Macon, Fort (So. Caro.), 17
Magruder, General John, 60
Major, General James P., 35
Malvern Hill, Battle of, 54, 56
Manassas, Battle of (First), 44
Manassas, Battle of (Second), 57
Marcy, Captain Randolph B., 36
Martí, ..., 31
Masó, ..., 31
Mason, Charles, 1, 15-16
Mason, Fort (Tex.), 37, 39-40
Meade, General George Gordon, 63, 65
Meade, Bishop William, 7, 50-51

Mechanicsville, Battle of, 54
Memminger, Christopher, 67
Molino del Rey, Battle of, 23
Monroe, Fort (Va.), 17, 19
Monterrey, Battle of, 22, 28
Mule Shoe Salient, 55-56
Murfreesboro, Battle of (See Stone's River)

— Mc —

McClellan, General George B., 8, 19, 46, 51-52, 54
McClellan's Peninsular Campaign, 45, 51, 54, 57
McPherson, Cadet John B., 33

— N —

9th U. S. Infantry Regiment, 34
Nitre (Nitre and Mining) Corps, 60
North Carolina Railroad, 61
Northrop, General Lucius B., 60

— O —

Oak Grove, Battle of, 54
Okeechobee, Battle of, 21-22
Old Point Comfort (Va.), 17

— P —

Palo Alto, Battle of, 22
Paulus Hook, Battle of, 13
Pedregal (At the Battle of Contreras), 2, 5, 25-26
Pegram, Colonel John, 33, 46, 56, 58
Pemberton, General John C., 45, 49
Pender, General Dorsey, 33, 58
Pendleton, General S. N., 64
Petersburg Troop of Cavalry, 23
Pettigrew, General James J., 66
Philippi, Battle of, 46

Pickens, Governor Francis W., 48, 50
Pickett, General George, 64-66
Piedmont Railroad, 61
Pierce, General/President Franklin, 15, 24, 26, 34
Pillow, General Gideon, 29, 59
Plattsburg, Battle of, 18
Poague, Captain W. T., 57
Polk, President James K., 27
Pope, General John, 54
Porter, General Fitz John, 33, 52, 54
Port Republic, Battle of, 27

— Q —

Queenstown Heights, Battle of, 18, 23
Quitman, General John A., 27, 31

— R —

Ramseur, General Stephan D., 56
Reagan, John, 67
Resaca de la Palma, Battle of, 22
Reynolds, General Joseph J., 6, 47
Richmond (Lee's horse), 56
Richmond and Danville Railroad, 11, 61-62
Rich Mountain, Battle of, 46
Riley, Lieutenant Colonel Bennett, 26
Rockbridge Artillery, 57, 59
Root, Elihu, 33
Rosecrans, General William S., 47
Rust, Colonel Albert, 6-7

— S —

St. John, General Isaac M., 10, 60-62
Santa Anna, General Antonio López, 20, 22, 25-26
Savage's Station, Battle of, 54
Sayler's Creek, Battle of, 58

Scott, General Winfield, 2, 4, 18, 22-27, 40-43, 59
2nd U. S. Cavalry Regiment, 3, 34-35, 39
2nd U. S. Dragoons, 36
Sedgwick, General John, 63
Seven Days' Battles, 53-54, 57
Seven Pines, Battle of, 8, 45, 51-52
7th U. S. Infantry Regiment, 21
Sharpsburg, Battle of, 10, 57, 59
Shenandoah Valley Campaign, 57
Sheridan, Cadet Phillip, 33
Sherman, General Thomas W., 48
Sherman, General William T., 45, 60
Shields, General James, 2, 26-27, 34
Shiloh, Battle of, 60
Sickles, General Daniel, 64
Smith, General E. Kirby, 35, 52
Smith, General Gustavus W., 51
Smith, General Persifor S., 2, 26, 28-29
Snelling, Fort (Minn.), 21
Spotsylvania, Court House, Battle of, 55
Stephen, Alexander, 67
Stoneman, General George, Jr., 35
Stone's River, Battle of, 60
Stuart, General James Ewell Brown, "JEB", 33, 37-38, 58, 65
Sumner, General E. V., 40
Sumter, Fort (So. Caro.), 19, 27

— T —

Tarleton, Colonel Banastre, 13
Taylor, Colonel W. H., 62, 67
Taylor, General/President Zachary, 1-2, 19-23, 32
Taylor's Battery, 28

10th U. S. Infantry Regiment, 34, 36
Texas Secession Convention, 39
The Roan (Lee's horse), 56
3rd Arkansas Infantry Regiment, 6
3rd U. S. Infantry Regiment, 21, 28
3rd U. S. Infantry Rifle Regiment, 28
13th Georgia Infantry Regiment, 56
13th U. S. Infantry Regiment, 18
Thomas, General George H., 33, 35, 37
Throckmorton, James "Old Leathercoat," 39
Totten, General Joseph G., 18, 25, 35
Traveller (Lee's horse), 25, 49, 55-56
Trumbull, Governor Lyman, 27
Twiggs, General David E., 28, 39-40
Tyler, President John, 18

— U —

United States Military Academy, 3, 4, 13-15, 18, 24, 30, 32-33, 44
Utah, Department of, 29, 36
Utah, Expedition to, 3, 35-36

— V —

Valencia, General Gabriel, 25-26
Vanderbilt, Cornelius, 67
Van Dorn, General Earl, 35
Venable, Colonel Charles, 55
Vera Cruz Army, 25
Vicksburg Campaign, 45, 60
Virginia Secession Convention, 41
Voltigeur Regiment, 29

— W —

Walker, Fort (So. Caro.), 48
Walker, Leroy P., 40
Warren, General G. K., 64
Washington (Washington and
  Lee) College, 58
Washington, General George,
  9, 13, 24
Western Virginia Campaign,
  45-48
West Point (See U. S. Military
  Academy)
Wise, General Henry, 46
Whiskey Rebellion (1794), 14
Whistler, Cadet James Mc-
  Neill, 33
White, Colonel ...., 31

Whiting, General W. H. C., 53
White Oak Swamp, Battle of,
  54
Wilcox, General Cadmus, 66
Wilderness, Battle of The,
  55-56
Williams, Dr. Kenneth P., 65
Williams, Captain Seth, 33
Winchester, Battle of, 27
Wood, 2nd Lieutenant Robert
  C., 34
Wool, General John Ellis, 1,
  18-20
Worth, General William J.,
  20, 31

— Y —

Yorktown, Siege of, 13